WINES OF PASSION

The BEST *of South America*

FRANKLIN REIDER'S

WINES OF PASSION
The BEST of South America

A CONNOISSEUR'S GUIDE TO THE FINEST
WINES OF ARGENTINA AND CHILE

authorHOUSE®

AuthorHouse™
1663 Liberty Drive
Bloomington, IN 47403
www.authorhouse.com
Phone: 1-800-839-8640

First published by AuthorHouse 1/11/2010

ISBN: 978-1-4490-6428-0
Library of Congress Control Number: 2009914362

Printed in the United States of America
Bloomington, Indiana

Back cover picture taken in the award-winning wine room of GOL!
The Taste of Brazil restaurant in Delray Beach, Florida

This book is printed on acid-free paper.

Acknowledgements

There are many people who were crucial in helping me learn about wines and specifically the wines of South America.

Gabriel Chagas took my hand some 30 years ago and introduced me to the marvels of first growth French wines. Many Brazilian friends, too numerous to mention, generously invited me to attend fabulous wine dinners over the decades.

Antonio Carlos Sequeira Castro presented me with my first Montes Alpha wine. Wilson Borges gave me my first Casa Silva Carmenere. Arthur Bellis generously shared his 1982 Petrus copiously.

After opening my restaurant, GOL! The Taste of Brazil, in Delray Beach, Florida, numerous wine merchants introduced me to the pleasures of fabulous wines from South America.

I want to thank the many people who reviewed parts of the book including Rich and Carol Pollack, Alicia Lammersdorf, Brian and Jessica Pilar Goldman, Andrew and Roxana Reider, Gregory and Ana Reider, Marcelo Rabelo, numerous other friends and family members.

Thanks go to Wines of Argentina and Wines of Chile for helping with access to the wineries and other sources of information, most especially Nora Favelukes, Maria Jimenez, Lori Tieszen, Andre Libeer.

Joao Pires Junior was especially helpful as well as so many people at Author House, including Adalee Cooney, Joe Scaggs, John Parsons and Terry Dwyer.

A special thanks to my children who are simultaneously my inspiration and my idols.

Contents

How Wine Found Me   1

A Metaphor For Life And Love   4

The Danger of Sameness   7

Terroir   9

The Issue of Age   10

Andes Mountains and Irrigation   11

Phylloxera   13

Winemaking: How Does It Happen?   15

Organic, Biodynamic and Sustainable Wine Practices   18

Malbec: The Wine that is Conquering the World Market   21

Carmenere: The Lost Grape of Bordeaux   24

Torrontes   26

Bonarda   27

Pinot Noir   28

Wine Labeling and Classifications   30

Analysis And Criteria   31

Argentina   33
    The Wines   *39*

Chile   123
    The Wines   *130*

Wine Tourism – Argentina   195

Wine Tourism – Chile   199

HOW WINE FOUND ME

*F*rom the time I started to have my own personality, the two things I cared the most about were sports and girls. I never drank alcohol nor did any type of drugs. {For my high school prom, I drank milk just to emphasize that I did not drink alcohol. In a film I saw, a cowboy ordered milk in a saloon and I thought that was one of the coolest things ever}.

At college, everyone did at least beer, most smoked pot and many tried acid. I sipped ginger ale. There were no moral issues here. I just did not like the taste of alcoholic beverages and drugs were just too risky in my view.

In law school, at NYU in the village, I found Dom Perignon and that was my rare drink of choice. On a date in my last year of law school, I took my future first wife to a wonderful French restaurant and we had a bottle of Dom Perignon and fell in love.

In the Peace Corps in Brazil, I discovered German-style Brazilian beer and the traditional Caipirinha. Later, single malt Scotch and Napoleon Cognac followed.

Wine? Nada.

In my early 30s, while living in Rio de Janeiro, my best Brazilian friend, Gabriel Chagas, decided to broaden my horizons and introduced me to Bordeaux wine, with an occasional Burgundy thrown in. I was hooked. I did not know that the wines I was drinking were beyond the normal pocket book. Lafitte Rothschild, Chateau Margaux, and Leoville Las Cases, among others, were the names that I cut my proverbial molars on. It was then I learned the pleasure of sharing wines with friends and making new friends over shared wines.

On a trip to visit my father in Florida, a drinker of Dewars scotch his entire adult life, I became friendly with Arthur Bellis, a collector of Petrus. He had sold his company and bought a significant number of cases of Petrus as an investment. On this trip, we had three bottles of the 1982 vintage. These experiences opened my eyes to what I had been missing and I began to explore the world of wines.

As the years went by, I developed what most people would consider a rather sophisticated palate. Blessed with a sensitive nose, I was able to distinguish significant characteristics of the grape prior to tasting. I am rather instinctive in my tastes and preferences and have not read or studied wine cultivation. I learned from drinking it.

The most pleasure in wine is the sharing it with friends or recent arrivals in my life who enjoy trying different wines. Laughter, stories, romance, excitement – they are all part of wine and the enjoyment thereof.

In 2006, I took the drastic step of opening a Brazilian steakhouse in Delray Beach Florida. GOL! The Taste of Brazil was born and I spent months developing the wine list on my own. When I started, I intended to do what all up-scale Brazilian steakhouses do – build a great wine cellar with fine French and European wines, complemented by a smattering of American and Australian wines. But something happened along the way.

The wine distributors came in by the dozens and the new and different wines by the hundreds. I discovered rating and *Wine Spectator* and Robert Parker and his wine advocate franchise.

The Margaux and the other Bordeaux that the wine distributors had were too young to be properly enjoyed. So I put my own French wines that were appropriately aged in GOL!'s wine cellar and proceeded to purchase wines at more reasonable cost that could be enjoyed without being aged, along with the wonderful meats and shrimp that dominate GOL!'s menu.

And along came Malbec from Argentina and, shortly thereafter, Carmenere from Chile. I put together a wonderful collection of European wines, but soon the strong Euro made even modest Italian wines difficult to price. On the other hand, the governments of Argentina and Chile discovered the foreign exchange value of exporting wines and the United States became their primary target.

It turned out that the prestigious French vineyards had discovered the potential in Latin America and had made major investments there. In Argentina, Lafitte Rothschild had established a joint venture with Argentina's largest wine producer, Catena, and the Caro Vineyard was born (the name Caro was formed from the first two letters of each partner). Similarly. Lafitte created Los Vascos and invested with Concha Y Toro in a single grand cru vineyard, Almaviva

Caro produces two outstanding wines, both blends of Malbec and Cabernet Sauvignon; the high-end Caro has all the power and taste of a Bordeaux, as does its little brother Amancaya. The latter costs less than $15 and is truly one of the great wine steals in the world. It accompanies steak with a fabulous complexity and body. Los Vascos had a slow start but today has magnificent wines. Almaviva, as we shall see, is in my opinion, one of the great wines of the world.

Among other international wine investments are Colome (Donald Hess), Vina Cobos (Paul Hobbs), Cheval Des Andes developed by Cheval Blanc, also a blend of Malbec and Cabernet Sauvignon, inter alia.

Casa Lapostelle of the Grand Marnier family, which produced Clos Apalta, *Wine Spectator's* wine of the year in 2008, is a fabulous success story and one of the most dramatic wineries I have ever seen.

We should emphasize that most of the great wineries of South America are established by native entrepreneurs of their country and are staffed by phenomenal winemakers born and educated at home. I do not want to offend the great families that have a tradition of making wonderful wines but leaders like Aurelio Montes in Chile and Nicolas Catena and Susana Balbo in Argentina represent a a class of dedicated, talented and brilliant winemakers that have been able to make wines using their native terroir and their artistic genius for establishing their countries as the fastest growing area of the world for great wines at accessible prices.

After discovering the history of Malbec and Carmenere, which is described in detail in later chapters, GOL! began to have a large collection of each, as I became more and more enamored of these grapes. Simultaneously, the wineries described herein began to separate their best produce to begin to compete with the top quality wines around the world.

Both countries still have mass-produced mediocre wines – no doubt. But the desire to be among the highest quality wines in the world is catching and both Chile and Argentina have entries in this league.

I have a special attachment to these wines as I grew in my ability to appreciate different wines as they grew in producing them. This book is intended to capture the coming of age of these wonderful wines and to help spread the word that the future is now for Latin American wines.

A METAPHOR FOR LIFE AND LOVE

*T*hroughout the ages, poets and writers of history have used wine as a metaphor for aspects of life. Cicero affirmed, "Men are like wine, age souring the bad and bettering the good."

Robert Louis Stevenson stated, "Wine is bottled poetry." My favorite, however, is from Martin Luther:

"He who loves not wine, women and song,
 He is a fool his whole life long."

Indeed, the appreciation of wine is a learned art, and concomitantly, with age, we learn how to enjoy aspects of life that – when younger – we did not even know existed. The question of how we learn to appreciate wine becomes a metaphor for how we learn to appreciate life and, in doing so, how we learn about love.

I began discovering the real pleasure of wines in my mid-30s. Friends invited me to join a wine club when I lived in Rio de Janeiro, and from there I began to develop a taste of my own. From wine, great friendships develop. And yes, in water one sees one's reflection but in wine one sees another's heart.

In so doing, we should learn to be adventurous when trying wines. Acquire a taste for what you like and go for it. Try new wines from around the world and remember the ones you like. Go back to them frequently to make sure you really enjoy them. One caveat: do not get stuck on what you have always liked; the more you experiment, the more your taste develops. I have found that some of the wines I loved 4 years ago do not hold the same pleasure any longer. With experience, we get more demanding. We learn and want to find that special something that we did not know existed when we were starting out. As it is true of love, so it is true of wine.

If you are serious about learning more, keep notes with your impressions and thoughts, as if you were keeping a diary. For the wines you find truly intriguing, remove the labels from the bottle and keep them in a book.

Like children taught by their parents, wine beginners are typically guided by the people who introduce them to wine, for better or worse. It is hoped that we go out on our own and find our way and our own private tastes. In the end, we like wines with upbringing, history and fine origins.

Through the years, I have developed a taste for French wine. In my opinion, Bordeaux wines are the standard against which all wines should be compared. There are many great wines produced in many other countries, but the depth and complexity of good or great French wine has been in a class by itself. Thus far, French wines are the sole wines that improve seemingly forever with age. And, their longevity truly distinguishes them from fine wines of most other countries.

The last time I traveled to Europe, I visited two of my favorite vineyards. Visiting a great winemaker is fascinating stuff and leads to an even greater appreciation of what they produce. I have found French wines have character and distinctive tastes; the longer they are opened, the more they bloom.

If you swirl them properly, they open and invite you for more pleasure – and they always leave you longing for more. A wine should do that. In my restaurant, when someone tells me the wine is nice, I think, hmm, OK. When they say, *"That is a great wine!"* I give them a high five!

Unfortunately, not all wine is produced with this dedication or inventiveness. Today, led by Australian and South African wines, (my opinion—there is no right and wrong here), too many winemakers and consumers are looking for wines that are unobjectionable. Their goal seems to be to achieve a wine that does not take risks; it sits in the glass (corner) and has little character, but does not do anything socially improper.

This approach is accentuated by a tendency for wine drinkers to be fearful to develop their own tastes, especially if they differ from others who supposedly are more learned in the subject. A high percentage of wine drinkers follow the crowd and buy what others rave about.

Many California wines are like this as well. Pinot Noir and Merlot get simpler and more bland every year. The good ones are very good, but very rare, and the majority are non-controversial and uninteresting.

Many consumers, where budget is not an object, go for the more expensive wine, thinking price will guarantee quality. In fact, in my experience, the major determinant of price is supply; many wines have a small number of cases produced each year, and therefore, are hard to find. Hence, the ability for winemakers to raise prices, under the perception that their wine is a rarity. If, through good marketing they create a demand for their product, the price will soar. As a result, price does not guarantee superior quality.

Some years ago, I read that Michael Jordan had dinner with his agent in the Presidential Suite of the Four Seasons in Chicago. When the sommelier asked him what wine he preferred, he answered: "The most expensive one." However, that is not how to drink wine.

The way to drink wine is to ask: Where is the charm? Where is the taste? Most of all, where is the adventure and the passion?

I love discovering new wines that surprise and excite me. I ask sommeliers for their best suggestions and why they chose them. Sommeliers who are serious about giving advice will make terrific recommendations. However, if they have a financial interest in selling certain wines, their opinion is useless. Figuring out where the truth lies is part of the adventure. If you do not see some passion in their advice, be wary.

Similarly, friends who discover great wines and want to share their finds, add another level to our friendship. When we share a truly magnificent wine, it is like a great conversation or intimate interaction. We get a feeling of exultation and *joie de vivre*.

Recently, a friend brought a fantastic Cabernet from Paul Schrader (of California) for a dinner as a surprise. We had a wonderful dinner, great conversation and lots of laughter. But the glue that brought us together was the generosity of an extra-special wine that symbolized his friendship and desire to bring pleasure to our time together.

As Mark Twain said, "There are no standards in wine." Each man's taste is his own standard. We must all develop our tastes through experimentation and curiosity.

So you might ask, "What should we drink that may not be French and will not break our bank, but will leave us longing for more?"

Latin America is the true new world for fabulous wines at great prices. Always considered part of the developing world, in wines as well, it is producing new labels with great value and quality. When I think of pleasure, I think of Latin America: Very sensuous and exciting. Latin culture never gets old. As in so many other aspects of Latin America, good wine has taken longer to be discovered but it is certainly worth the wait.

To prove a point, I went to the Wine Spectator Experience, where South America, for the first time, had a significant presence with almost five percent of the wines present. I tasted the great French Bordeaux wines, my lifetime favorites, against the best of Chile and Argentina. I must say that South American beauties stood up well against the unquestionable world leaders from France.

Lafitte Rothschild had two Latin wines and they were fantastic. Lafitte is one of my favorites and Caro, its Argentine representative and about 1/5 the price, was as deep and provoking and delicious as its French parent. Almaviva, Lafitte's Chilean star may have been the best wine there, hence the best wine in the world. So here's to life, love and discovering them with fine South American wines!!

THE DANGER OF SAMENESS

*I*n tasting new wines almost weekly with distributors, I have found on the one hand, there are truly a plethora of enjoyable wines. I have also noted that there are a growing number of consultants, usually French, who are advising wineries all over the world.

What has happened is that science has invaded the winemaking process, much like how science can improve computer chips year after year. We would like to think that wine is not a computer chip, that wine is individual and distinctive – that like snow flakes, there is always something different about each one that eliminates sameness and creates fascination.

Most importantly, I believe winemaking is an art, not a science, with the creativity and individuality of the winemaker being the key to the success of the wine.

Unfortunately, the trend is toward sameness. The consultants have found how to make agreeable wine from virtually any grape. So if the land is cheap and the labor is cheap, why not make a wine equal to that in Napa but at 10% of the cost.

Add great marketing and a strong distributor and you cannot go wrong. This is the brave new world of winemaking and we have it today in abundance. I defy the cognoscenti of wine degustation to differentiate the Chardonnay from the west coast of the United States from those of Australia or South Africa or many from Latin America and Europe. Too often it cannot be done because in more and more cases, there are no differences.

That is not to say that they are not tasty. That is to say that they are not different. They are not unique. There is an old saying that people get the government they deserve. That is becoming truer of wines as well. Great vineyards must take risks. They must maintain uniqueness. This book looks for those wines and intends to point them out and hope true aficionados will help in this search.

What happens is that the "consultants" have their oaking procedures and other touches that smooth out their wines. Many wines are harsh. The prime harvesting times are difficult to judge for many grapes.

The more complex the grape, the more one needs an experienced winemaker to determine when the time is right. The consultants take away all that risk but their systems are the same all over, and once wine is 24 months in oak, a lot of defects go away. Does that mean that they will all taste the same? Not necessarily but the risk increases dramatically. There are many other aspects of winemaking, for sure.

After visiting some 60 wineries in Chile and Argentina, I am happy to say there are many wineries striving to keep their identity and emphasize their terroir. There are creative winemakers, both homegrown in Mendoza and Chile, as well as internationally trained, who are making creative and artistic wines that are simply delicious and faithful to the origins of their grapes.

Not only are the Malbecs and the Carmeneres flourishing, but also there are wonderful white wines that exploit the terrific contrasts in temperatures, the cold Pacific winds, the fogs and the pure water of the Andes to make their individualistic versions of wines made all over the world.

Let us praise the wines that courageously offer up a tropical taste, maximizing the rich, fruity strains found in the Southern Hemisphere. Herein, we will examine those artistic winemakers and their creations and exalt those who are constantly striving for the unattainable –perfection- and the many who come very close!

TERROIR

*T*erra is the Latin word for land. Today, it is still common usage in many romance languages, including Spanish.

In French wine circles, terroir is the individuality that each vineyard has, or should have, produced by the particulars of its land, its grapes, its cultivation, and its fermentation process that we hope does not obfuscate all of the above.

In fact, unfortunately, most vineyards around the world attempt to satisfy the most mediocre of tastes in order to increase sales to the largest public and the terroir that years of growth could have developed, is destroyed by the attempt to achieve sameness.

Terroir is individuality, per se. Much of Burgundy and Bordeaux, the most famous of wine-growing areas in France, and the world for that matter, strive to maintain the concept of terroir, even at great cost.

The concept of terroir is widely debated among wine aficionados. The pro terroir side (Robert Parker's sly name for the group is terroiristes) proclaims that to be a great wine, terroir is a *sine qua non.*

The individuality that terroir produces must be maintained at all costs. The most extreme of this group rejects even filtration as being unacceptable taste altering. The basic concept is that "less is more", i.e., nature makes the wine, with an inherent taste, and it is man's job to let that come out. It is forbidden for man to create wine; he is there to protect what nature has wrought. The French take pride in wines that are *sauvage,* the Italians have their *rusticos.*

Man eliminates nothing from the natural process and let the dice fall where they may. Some potentially great wines can be hurt by letting nature take its way; sometimes it is financially disastrous. But for those who believe in terroir in extremis, the final product is divine.

Then there are those who believe in terroir but also believe that there are impurities and/or defects that should be corrected; that sometimes the wines become too natural, almost hard in nature and unattractive. Beautiful models are improved by plastic surgery, why not wines?

The answer, say the purists, is that eliminating imperfections eliminates individuality, creates sameness, which ends up in uniform taste and, finally boredom.

For me, I hope that the New World will be able to imitate the idols of the French market and maintain its individuality. As we will see, the Andes Mountains and the climates of Chile and Argentina are *sui generis* and totally different from any locales elsewhere in the world.

As a result, the tannins are different, the skins of the grapes are different and the entire process is longer, which results in a different product. How will terroir affect the wines of Latin America? We will examine this in detail, vineyard by vineyard.

THE ISSUE OF AGE

When one discovers the marvels of having a 1982 Chateau Margaux, savoring the complexities and depth of the taste, appreciating the wonderful finish that leaves such a sensual residual taste in one's mouth, one has to wonder why anyone drinks young wines.

But the fact is, perhaps surprisingly, that most wines do not age well in bottles. Most wines that taste good soon after being bottled, do not taste better ten years later. In fact, most wines taste worse ten years later.

Furthermore, after a certain period of time, most bottled wines start turning into vinegar. So if we think of investing in wines, or just cellaring wines we like for future enjoyment, we have to choose wisely or be unpleasantly surprised when we open a bottle of wine 13 years later to celebrate a child's achievement with a bottle from the year of his birth.

Great Bordeaux wines and many other European wines have gotten deserved fame because they get better with age. The thrill of drinking a wonderful wine from a great year decades after it has been bottled is unforgettable for many of us. Margaux Hemmingway got her name from the wine her parents drank the night she was conceived.

Irrefutably, great European wines get better with age and represent great investments for both financial and pleasure purposes. But do other fine wines improve with age? More particularly, do South American wines get better with age?

In some cases we just do not yet know. But here are some guidelines:

A wine that is bad and rough when opened probably will always be so, no matter how old it gets. Wines that are good but taste young, so to speak, can and may well improve with aging up to a point. Both Carmenere and Malbec wines are grown to be enjoyed fairly young. Carmenere was only discovered in Chile in the 1990's as not being another form of Merlot, so it does not have the history to prove how it will age. Clearly, it is a complex grape, requiring time to breathe after being opened, regardless of age. This is a characteristic of Bordeaux wines and the good pure Carmeneres have a distinct and complex taste after being decanted and breathing for a while. There is a harshness initially after the bottle is open that totally disappears after 20-40 minutes in most of the quality Carmeneres.

In the subsequent reviews herein, I mention specifically wines that I have verified age well. Many Malbecs and Malbec blends have shown to improve with aging over a 7-10 year period. Some seem to have the characteristics that indicate further aging will help the wine further develop. The Icons of Achaval Ferrer, Catena, Caro, Concha y Toro, Alma Viva, Cheval des Andes, Los Vascos, Altair and a number of others give every indication of terrific aging potential. To say they will improve after 10 years!? Even the winemakers have told me they have no certainty yet.

ANDES MOUNTAINS AND IRRIGATION

$\mathcal{T}$he Andes are the world's longest mountain range, stretching over seven countries, starting in Venezuela and extending 6000 miles down to the Southern tip of South America and Tierra del Fuego. With 30 spectacular volcanoes still active, the Andes present some of the most diverse natural habitats in the world.

In Southern Chile, there are magnificent glaciers. Deserts, lush grasslands and high altitude lakes are among the most varied of the microclimates. Lake Titicaca is the highest large navigable lake in the world. The Andes are higher than the Rocky Mountains, losing only to the Himalayas worldwide.

But for our purposes, the Andes supply one of the essential factors for great wines: pure and abundant water. Since early civilizations, the occupants of what are now Chile and Argentina had insignificant rainfall and most of their land was desert. The essential water for life had to be captured and saved from the meltdown of snow off the magnificent Andes.

Throughout the history of the countries bordering the Andes, governments were made and overturned by using the control of the water systems built around the Andes water sources. The Incan empire was forged on its development of the canals and irrigation systems throughout South America. The systems used in both Chile and Argentina today are based on the infrastructure developed by the Incan empire. Today, an intricate system of channels, dams, and canals allows the governments to offer pure and abundant water year round to the desert areas, forming oases ideal for viticulture farming, including the fabulous vineyards in both countries.

With the alluvial soils being mostly sandy with areas of clay and stones, the vines must be strong to seek out the water below. The rugged terrain leads to healthy, more vibrant vines, which in turn produce fuller and juicier grapes.

The key to these vines producing the valued grapes essential for premium wines is the water control. Earlier stages of wine production used flooding to produce mammoth quantities of unexciting bulk wine. Economically rewarding, it was meaningless from the oenologists' goals.

When premium wines became important, the study of how to best monitor irrigation became a major factor. Many of the top wineries, both domestic and international, quickly discovered that careful control of the water combined with extremely low yields of high quality grapes produced the flavor and intense varietal character essential to premium wines. In the last two decades, experiments with finely controlled water supply have led to mastering the issues that the market demanded and leading to the production of dramatically increased quality.

Higher "hang time," to use a popular expression among winemakers, is created by controlling the amount of water available to the vines, resulting in "a greater accumulation of aromas, full maturation of tannins and a better balance between sugar and acidity" (Catena winery).

Iconic Winemaker Nicolas Catena goes on to say, "Strict irrigation control leads to an enormous leap in grape quality and … after 20 years we know more about irrigation management than any other viticulture operation worldwide."

This writer believes he speaks for many wineries in Chile and Argentina.

PHYLLOXERA

A horrible insect that attacks the roots of vines, Phylloxera periodically destroys entire regions of wine throughout most of the world. A small, yellow insect, this aphid has caused more damage to great vineyards than any other natural phenomena in history. It kills the vine by eating away at the roots and can destroy entire regions.

In 1863, it spread across Bordeaux wreaking havoc throughout the great vineyards. It was at this time that Chilean importers took the now-famous Carmenere grape to Chile, where it flourished as a Merlot variation. Similarly, large landowners in Argentina brought over European vines, with the emphasis being Cabernet Sauvignon and Malbec from Southern France.

Apparently, the Phylloxera insect came from America, where it had already caused damage and still does periodically. In France, 6.2 million acres (2.5 million hectares) were destroyed. The future of French wine was clearly threatened at this time, and it was somewhat of a miracle it recovered.

The greatest problem of this insect is that it is virtually invisible to the naked eye, as it lays millions of eggs around the roots of the grape vines. Furthermore, because they are so small a strong wind carries them to neighboring areas and they spread unmercifully. For whatever reason, the mid 1860s was the time that vineyards all over Europe and the United States were attacked by this plague.

Humans have played a large part in the spreading of Phylloxera by bringing roots from one country to another for planting, not knowing that the insect is attached. They are then spread by wind, water, tractors and other means without anyone being conscious of what is happening.

Phylloxera has never been present in Argentina and Chile. The governments of each country can take credit as they forbid the importation of more roots once Phylloxera took hold in the United States and Europe. Some scientists also attribute the Andes and its climate as a reason for the insect never taking hold. Cynics say it is just blind luck. For whatever reason, this dreaded disease has omitted Latin America from its list of victims, much to the benefit of these countries' wine industry.

Fortunately, by the 20th century this plague had ceased to be a threat to vineyards, as a wide range of rootstocks is now resistant to the bug. By 1990, scientists believe some 85 percent of rootstocks around the world are resistant to the disease. However, there were attacks in the 1980s in California, New Zealand, Greece and Australia, among others.

Although today Phylloxera is not a serious threat, both Argentina and Chile have benefited from France's misfortune, as the French Carmenere and Malbec have flourished in Latin America.

Additionally, when the wineries of Europe were threatened in the 1860s, many talented winemakers and other workers migrated to South America in search for work. The great microclimates of the Southern part of the continent welcomed this skilled labor and many new vineyards were planted. Their families grew and many vineyards are still worked by generations of their offspring.

WINEMAKING: HOW DOES IT HAPPEN?

*H*ow do grapes become wine? This is not the place for a detailed scientific explanation. But it is important to know the basics because we want to know whether the wine is mass produced or has some character that will help it develop over time into something extraordinary. Here are some issues that some consumers might want to know about their favorite wines:

Basically, making the wine is the process of turning the sugar held in the grape into alcohol. Since the ancient Iran of 2700 BC, wine has been made by such a process. Whether the stems are removed or not, whether the skins are present for the entire process or for a shorter period of time, all of the details add to the individuality of each wine and each region.

Let us hope each has traditions that work and that are handed down from generation to generation. As time goes by, these traditions have a tendency to drop by the wayside, supposedly to improve the quality, but usually for financial reasons. Generally, the altering of the process has reduced the individuality of the wine in question.

What is added and subtracted from the grapes during this process is crucial to the end product. Is sugar added? What is done with acidity? Does the producer want more or less tannin? Is it aged in barrels that affect the final taste? If so, how does the real character of the wine come forth and does it at all?

Acidity, for instance, is crucial in how a wine tastes. Malic acid is found in grape juice and other fruits. In apples, it gives the fruit a certain tartness. Most white wines have this characteristic to varying degrees and often determine whether the taste is pleasing or not.

In red wines, malic acid can be very disagreeable and therefore winemakers take the grapes through a second fermentation: malo-lactic fermentation. This softens the acidity to acceptable levels, similar to dairy fermentation. How this is carried out is a very important determinant of the final taste of the wine.

Once this is completed, the wine may or may not be aged, which is where oak treatment of the wine enters. The choices of expensive French oak barrels, new or used, American in part, number of months – all of these options the winemaker must determine.

All involve significant costs. French oak taste is more pronounced, newer oak is stronger than used, American oak gives more of a vanilla flavor, etc. Tannins are affected by the type of oak used and the amount of time the wine is aged in barrels. The amount of time the wine is in contact with the skins is very important in tannin development.

These issues make up an entire university education, so I do not presume to explain them here. I raise them for the reader to be aware of what they are and to understand what is meant when they are referred to in the evaluation of each wine. There are many books devoted to these subjects for those who want to go into greater depth.

Another crucial issue: Is there blending with other grapes or other vineyards? To be classified as a particular grape, each country has its own rules and the associations can be more or less strict in enforcing them.

If a particular year is negatively affected by the weather, will the product be mixed with a different grape to achieve a satisfactory result that is saleable? Or will that year be skipped partially or altogether to maintain the quality of the name for future years? These are difficult financial and cultural questions that come up much more frequently than the public realizes.

The issue of oak aging is crucial to the individuality of the wine and the maintenance of the wines terroir. In my opinion, the better wineries in Latin America, unlike other parts of the New World, have maintained great balance in their use of oak aging.

Judicious use of new French oak can give a wonderful roundness and structure to a terrific wine, while maintaining its individuality. Over-oaking can make a tasty wine, but cause it to lose its individuality and taste like a wine with totally different grapes from another county. If a Syrah from France has the same taste as a Malbec from Argentina, usually it can be attributed to the over usage of oak aging. This is very undesirable, even if the wine ends up selling well.

The wines of South America are privileged to have a wonderful climate that enables greater hang time than just about any location in the world. The big, juicy reds that result should be applauded and their individuality maintained.

A wonderful Carmenere or a strong masculine Malbe needs to keep its individuality and thrust. It may be smooth like a wonderful Bordeaux but the wine should have its own taste and terroir. Many do, as we will see in our evaluations. The world will discover them more and more each year. We must reward and encourage this individuality. As an example of such magnificent work, I will refer to some of the now internationally recognized successes from South America.

At a recent *Wine Spectator* tasting, I was privileged to drink many of my favorite First Growth Bordeaux wines as well as many other top quality wines from around the world. For the first time, Argentina and Chile had significant representation.

I compared Chateau Margaux to Almaviva (Chile), Cheval Blanc to Clos Apalta (Chile), Lafitte Rothschild to its Argentine spin-off Caro, Pichon Longueville to Don Melchor (Chile), Sassicaia to Trapiche's single vineyard Malbec and Caymus to Nosotros (Argentina). Although the average price of the Latin wine was only 25 percent of the European, the taste of the Latin wines was as good or better than the adversary's.

Additionally, and perhaps most importantly, the taste of the Latin wines respected their heritage and their terroir. The oaking was appropriate; the taste of the tropical grapes maintained, if not glorified. The Latin wines were delicious but tropical. Getting these wines to be better known is my personal goal.

Other fabulous Latin representations were:

Alto from Altavista (Argentina); Single Vineyard Malbec from Achaval Ferrer (Argentina), Catena Zapata Malbec (Argentina), Alfa Cruz from O. Fournier (Argentina) and Montes M (Chile).

All of these wines are reviewed herein and would be excellent additions to experts' wine cellars or for beginners. I believe they all are age worthy and have retained the true terroir of their country. Most cost around $60 and all are under $100.

ORGANIC, BIODYNAMIC AND SUSTAINABLE WINE PRACTICES

South American wineries have become very conscious of producing wines in a manner that respects the environment and reduces the carbon footprint of the processing of grapes.

Sustainable practices are becoming the norm for most of the wineries. In Chile and Argentina, the various microclimates make this process easier. High altitudes and pure water from the Andes eliminates many of the risks that require pesticides and other chemical usage.

Below are some definitions of terms used in the description of the wineries throughout this book. I relied on an excellent presentation from Emiliana winery for most of the definitions herein. Emiliana is the largest organic winery in the world and is one of Chile's most important.

CONVENTIONAL AGRICULTURE

Agrochemicals are used as a first resort in treating problems. Frequently, chemicals are used preemptively and in a programmed fashion. No thought is given to the ecological impact of these policies.

SUSTAINABLE POLICIES

Agrochemicals are used only when necessary and are avoided whenever possible. There is no legal definition with this concept; it is an attitude, an approach to eliminating chemical implementation. The University of California, Davis, uses the following definition: *meet the needs of the present without compromising the ability of future generations to meet their own needs.* Most of the wineries I have visited in Argentina and Chile use this philosophy, at the very least. Many of the farms and wineries farm organically entirely or in great part, but retain the flexibility of being able to use what works best for their individual properties when they deem it necessary. Clearer standards are being developed, as sustainable policies are very important and need to be defined and certified to encourage their greater use.

INTEGRATED PRODUCTION

IP is the how of sustainability. Herbicides, pesticides and fertilizers can be used if all other alternatives have been exhausted. IP sees the vineyard as an "agro-ecosystem" of interconnected parts. The vineyard should be in harmony with its animals and plants and, in turn, these surrounding ecosystems can be high quality grapes. In so doing, the native 'terroir' is enhanced by these purer systems.

Trees are replanted instead of cut down; in so doing, birds and other animals do not lose their native habitat and aid in controlling pests. Knowledge of local animals and life cycles of plants and bio-culture is integrated into the decision-making process of how to produce the best wines from the plantations.

ISO 14001

ISO 14001 is a builder's manual on how to establish Environmental Management Systems (EMS) and was created by the International Organization for Standardization, ISO, which is based in Geneva, Switzerland.

ISO sets strict and specific requirements on what the monitoring procedure must look like. Receiving an ISO 14001 award means the company has been externally audited by accredited examiners and proven that it has set up an EMS in compliance with the requirements. Many wineries in South America have taken the steps to do this, Emiliana and Colome among them. Many of these wineries are identified in their descriptions herein.

ORGANIC

Industrial chemicals, synthetic pesticides, herbicides and fungicides, chemical or sewage sludge-based fertilizers are prohibited. Typically, accreditation and inspection are administered by independent assessors. Genetically modified organisms are prohibited.

Waste material from the winery, grape seeds, stems and skins, will be recycled into fertilizer. For wineries, most chemical additives, especially synthetic fining agent PVPP, are prohibited. However, because of the high risk of bacterial spoilage, some sulfur dioxide is used. The level usually is about two-thirds the amount permitted for conventional wine producers.

BIODYNAMICS

Here there are three basic tenets: A closed ecosystem -- all that is used inside is produced inside. Homeopathic concepts are followed. The moon calendar is determinant.

Keeping soil healthy is a basic concept to prevent disease. Feeding organic manure to the plantations, albeit with a small booster of homeopathic medicine, is the best way to maintain healthy vines. Six different boosting preparations are made from yarrow, chamomile, dandelion and valerian flowers, oak bark and stinging nettle.

Additionally, there are three preparations that are sprayed directly on the vines: horn manure 500, horn silica 501, and common horsetail 508. There are a variety of other technical applications that obey divisions of the calendar to take into consideration the position of the moon, sun, planets, inter alia. In so doing, aspects such as gravitational pull from the position of the moon may determine the best time to apply these techniques.

Accredited biodynamic certifying organizations verify that the winery has not used synthetic chemicals for three years and has used biodynamic preparations exclusively for two years in order to be classified as biodynamic.

The U.S. Government regulates the use of the term "organic", but sustainable and bio-dynamic have no legal definitions. There are 2 types of organic listings on wine bottles for the U.S. First, certified organic grapes which do not use any synthetic additives in their farming. Second, "organic wines" are made from organically grown grapes and are made without any added sulfites, although naturally occurring sulfites may be present.

As indicated above, I believe that using Sustainable procedures is the most important policy change needed at this point. As this process is better defined and the government establishes a definition therefore, I believe auditing agencies will give credibility and incentive for wineries to continue to adapt to this philosophy, as so many already have.

MALBEC: THE WINE THAT IS CONQUERING THE WORLD MARKET

$\mathcal{N}$ew developments have made the growth of Malbec, and its acceptance among the most demanding critics worldwide, one of the most compelling stories in recent wine history.

As an illustration, just in the year 2008, dollar sales of Malbec alone grew 43 percent over 2007, and volume (number of bottles sold) grew 37 percent in the same time period. Over 25 percent is sold to the United States. Argentina is now the fifth-largest wine producer in the world.

Many wine pundits attempt to make the Argentine story complex but in fact it is very simple. Although Argentina produces excellent Cabernet Sauvignon, as well as some other grapes, Malbec is THE story and Mendoza is THE region.

Argentina is the largest wine producer in South America. Historically, its population had one of the highest per capita consumption of wine in the world, on par with France. Now Argentina has an annual per capita consumption of over 30 liters, whereas the US is seven.

In the past, Argentine wines were produced and consumed early, with little or no aging. When foreign vineyards started entering the country, more serious wine was produced and the country began choosing its better grapes for export. Led by Catena, Argentina's largest local vineyard, quality took major leaps in the 1990's.

Today, Malbec and Malbec blends, principally with the Cabernet Sauvignon grape, are the leading growth wines in the world. As a result of the high internal consumption, Argentina has limited its exports to its highest quality wines, with most of the bulk production being consumed internally.

Mendoza is the second highest (in altitude) wine-producing region in Argentina and by far the largest region in terms of number of vineyards and in terms of quantity and quality of wine produced. Interestingly, an acre of wine country in Mendoza costs around $30,000, whereas in Napa Valley it is closer to $300,000.

One of the most curious aspects of wine producing in Argentina is that the vineyards benefit by high altitudes, some of the vineyards being as high as 9000 feet above sea level. Initially to me that was totally counterintuitive, with the great vineyards of France being at sea level or low altitude above the sea. Argentina is very far south in the Southern Hemisphere, and the winters are famous for skiing, with mountains not unlike those in Colorado.

However, one of the huge advantages of producing grapes at high altitudes in very fertile soil is that the skin of the grape becomes thicker and produces more tannins than grapes grown at a lower altitude. The water produced by the melting snow, in great quantity, is pure and makes the grapes richer and larger.

Hence, the taste of the wine produced seems, at times, to be more French than the French. That is, the wine is rich and deep, with wonderful plum taste, and it ages very well. Along this line, UV levels rise as the altitude increases, which apparently intensify carotenoids. The thicker skins produce more layers of cells, which result in greater aromatics and tannins.

With the low cost of land, the facility of excellent water and great climate, it is estimated that the costs of producing top quality wines in Mendoza is about 1/4 the cost in Napa or France

Though Malbec is originally from southern France, Bordeaux and Cahors, the wines produced in Argentina often have a Burgundy like strength, with the Cabernet being more Bordeaux-like.

Additionally, in the weak economy dominating the world markets, the sales of wines in quantity has dropped radically and it appears that this trend will continue. Similarly, the pressure to lower prices is huge. This places Argentina at a great advantage. The quality of its wines is improving, while their prices are low, so the price-conscious consumer anxiously goes after the "new" Malbecs, of which they are just becoming aware.

Truly, Malbecs and Malbec blends are becoming the wine of choice at the steak houses and barbeques around the United States. While the weak dollar has made European wines outrageously expensive for most consumers, the Argentine peso has weakened drastically compared to the US dollar in the last few years, making Argentine wine even more affordable.

Malbec hails originally from France, having grown in both Bordeaux and Cahors. In 1852, Don Miguel Aime Pouget, a Frenchman, was commissioned by then Argentine president, Sarmiento, to create an educational center in Mendoza.

Today, the Quinta Nacional graduates talented agricultural engineers that have made and continue to make Mendoza the young, vibrant wine center it is. The university propagated the first Malbec vines that Pouget obtained from France, called Uva Francesa or the French Grape.

The ravage of the Phylloxera, described herein, virtually ended the creation of Auxerrois, or the black wine of Cahors, as the French called Malbec. The dominance of Malbec in Argentina has varied, as many of the oldest vines were cloned into other grapes, either for ease in making bulk wines, or because foreign investors wanted other grapes like Cabernet Sauvignon or Petit Verdot in its place. But its resurgence in the last 20 years has once again put Malbec at the top of the "native" Argentinean grapes.

The character of the Argentinean version is quite different from its ancestors in France. Both have high tannin content, but while Argentina produces smooth-tasting grapes with velvety finishing, Cahors is known for its more rustic, harsher palate.

Many winemakers in Mendoza credit the superior taste of Argentina's Malbec to the Darwinian selection of the healthiest vines to withdraw the

Malbec clones from, thereby increasing the production and planting of new vineyards with better and better quality.

For instance, in the Uxmal vineyard in Agrelo, which pertains to the Catena Zapata group, the vines were planted from a scientific selection made in 1994. Judging upon criteria such as tannin quality, most concentrated fruit, and grapes that had the highest degree of even ripening, new clones were developed to make the best Malbec possible.

This type of work was done more frequently as new vineyards sprang up. Through this selection process, single vineyard, 100 percent Malbec wines have become the most in demand. Similarly, high quality blends that use these special cloned vines have become *icons,* the description for the winery's flagship brand.

Furthermore, the new definition of the terroir of each vineyard comes to the fore. Additionally, unusual climate of low humidity and sun exposure, combined with warm days and cool nights, allows for optimal maturation of the "new" Malbec.

CARMENERE: THE LOST
GRAPE OF BORDEAUX

*L*ike most wine lovers, I enjoy "discovering" new wines with wonderful tastes. The wine that has been the greatest discovery from opening GOL! The Taste of Brazil in 2006 is the Chilean wines made with Carmenere, a grape whose origin is a fascinating tale.

Chile has been producing wine since the 1500s when Spanish settlers brought over vines to plant in this Latin American country. Through a combination of great soil and weather, and a lot of luck, the country was able to remain disease free until today. In addition, Chile has become known for its Merlot and Cabernet Sauvignon, amongst their reds

In the 1860s France's Bordeaux region was devastated by an outbreak of Phylloxera, a horrendous aphid that attacks the roots of vinifera vines, the species of the great European grapes. Several million acres of vineyards across Europe were destroyed.

Similar tragedy hit the U.S. as well. Oddly, whether through luck, careful importation policies or the presence of the monumental Andes mountains separating Chile from the East, no such plague hit the plantations of the Chilean countryside.

Fortunately, this Bordeaux rootstock, Carmenere, Cabernet Sauvignon and Cabernet Franc, had been planted in Chile, disease free, some 30 years prior to the European plague.

When the French viniculturists replanted their grapes, Carmenere was not among those chosen. Strangely, Carmenere had been a difficult grape for the French environment, as it needed more heat than its counterparts, and even more problematic, it frequently caught "coulure," a disease that caused grapes to drop prior to their being ripe, thereby causing them to be useless for wine production. With such complications, Carmenere was discarded by the French.

However, Chile retains a wonderful climate, ideal for the longer ripening process that Carmenere requires. The fame that Chile's Merlot achieved, unknown to its creators, was in great part Carmenere. The Chilean winegrowers did not realize that Carmenere was a totally different grape from Merlot, not just a different variation version of the Merlot grape.

In 1994, Jean Michel Boursiquot, a visiting French ampelographist (an expert in identifying and distinguishing vines) from the Universite de Montpellier decided to investigate the Merlot plantings, and discovered the leaves of the Carmenere grape. Three years of DNA testing confirmed that Carmenere was alive and flourishing in Chile, in a manner superior to what it had ever done in France.

Many vineyards, when informed of this "new grape" present on their grounds for more than a century and a half, separated the plantings of Carmenere from

Merlot and the Chilean government encouraged the branding of Carmenere. The international community, led by the University of Montpellier, officially accepted Chile's Carmenere as a recognized wine category.

Initially, Carmenere continued to be blended with Cabernet and Merlot. Beginning around the turn of the 21sr century, Carmenere has begun to be bottled on its own and has developed into some wonderful wines.

In my personal opinion, the pure Carmenere can be somewhat irregular, with the same producer in the same year having bottles that are spectacular and others of the same vintage more ordinary. However, the latest vintages of pure Carmenere or predominantly Carmenere are reaching new plateaus of high quality.

The great wineries are now dominating the grape with very late harvest and moderate oak aging. Certainly, the choice of Clos Apalta as the 2008 Wine of the Year by Wine Spectator consecrated Carmenere as a high quality grape.

Clos Apalta is 61% Carmenere in its latest vintage and is truly a marvelous wine.

Below we will find fabulous Carmeneres. Please particularly note some of the best wines from Chile are now either Carmenere blends or pure Carmeneres. Wineries like Montes, Concha y Toro, and most especially, the iconic Almaviva have mastered the production of Carmenere and I believe there are some 20 truly fabulous Carmeneres that will be "discovered" in the years to come to be among the world's finest wines. All wine lovers should "discover" their favorite Carmenere. Let us be your guide right here.

TORRONTES

*T*orrontes is a white grape found almost exclusively in Argentina, and most successfully in the Salta region of the Northern mountains. Originally indigenous to Spain, it was brought to Argentina in the mid nineteenth century. Very little is found anymore in its homeland.

Torrontes had been used principally in bulk wine until the late 1990s when some wineries began making it as a varietal for export. It is not a simple wine, having more complexity than most whites and a very definitive character, which is not always pleasing. Torrontes is a cross between Moscatel and Criolla Chica.

Cafayate Valley near Salta has vineyards with altitudes of almost 9000 feet. These are skiing altitudes, such as are in Vail, Colorado, among others. It would seem counterintuitive to grow wines at such heights, but it turns out that the hot tropical sun and the pure mountain water makes for sturdy, high tannin, and delicious grapes that seem to fail in Mediterranean climates.

Torrontes is an example of such a grape. The sun is so strong in the winter that pergola vines have been grown to provide a leafy canopy to protect the grapes. Also, fungus and other diseases are almost unheard of at these altitudes so making biodynamic wines is the norm rather than the exception. Today, the important wineries of Argentina are producing wonderful varietals of Torrontes and exporting them in growing numbers around the world.

Torrontes has a definitive personality with lots of citrus, principally grapefruit, tones. Its color is a pale maize tone. There are influences of some sweeter fruit as well, such as apple and liche. There is clear minerality from the rocky soil giving it a very distinctive taste.

Torrontes when done correctly refreshes the palate and complements Thai food, sushi, and grilled seafood. Some versions are sweeter than others, rivaling Rieslings when young, and Chablis when aged longer.

Making this wine delicious is not for amateurs and many attempts have been too overwhelming in their fruitiness and acidity to please the international markets. However, today there are many talented winemakers making outstanding Torrontes wines with singular character and taste. Using skin contact, cold maceration, and oak aging to develop different touches and maturity, create new opportunities for Torrontes. We will see some 15 different products herein that are terrific.

I serve a variety of Torrontes in my restaurant and have found that many clients have adopted the Torrontes as favorites in lieu of Riesling, Chardonnay and Sauvignon Blanc.

I believe that Torrontes, within the next 10 years, will have become the beautiful sister of Malbec in the international markets and that it behooves the wineries of Argentina to bring this grape to the forefront much like they have done with Malbec itself.

BONARDA

Bonarda is a grape found in Argentina that historically has been used for bulk wine. A vine that is easy to grow and needs little tending, it has been ideal for the large, massive wines that dominated the internal markets for centuries.

However, Bonarda was discovered to blend well with Malbec and Cabernet Sauvignon and began to be treated with more respect in the last decade. Today, leading wineries such as Dominio del Plata, Catena and Trapiche have excellent pure Bonarda wines, as well as special blends, principally with Syrah. Many of the top wineries use small amounts of Bonarda with their top blends, often with Malbec.

The history of the grape is somewhat obscure. Most stories give its origin to Southern Italy. Some Argentine websites say it came from Bonarda Piemontese. This is incorrect, according to Susana Balbo, President of Wines of Chile. Its true origin is Western Europe, particularly the Savoie region of France, where it is called Charbonneau. It is also found in California under the name Charbono, where it has somewhat of a cult following. In Argentina, Bonarda had been the grape grown in the most hectares, until it was recently surpassed by Malbec. It continues to be the base for the large industry of bulk wines.

Bonarda, when cultivated for high quality, is a rustic wine, with strong, earthy tones. It is plump and full bodied, and has interesting tannins, giving it the potential for terrific wines. With these characteristics, it blends well with Syrah and other grapes that receive more potent grapes well.

Argentina's more creative wineries will be producing wonderful Bonardas at very reasonable prices in growing amounts in the upcoming years. Trapiche already has a very well priced Bonarda that I found outstanding.

PINOT NOIR

I must confess that my personal tastes run toward big, full-bodied red wines. Hence, I have never really enjoyed most Pinot Noir that I have come across, with the exception of the excellent product of Burgundy, which are much bigger than most.

The most popular Pinot Noir grapes are grown in climate and soil conditions that are propitious for terrific white wines, such as Chardonnay and Sauvignon Blanc. Not surprisingly Burgundy has wonderful whites such as Chablis and Pouilly Fuisse. Chile and Argentina grow their best Pinot Noir in the same regions that produce their best white wines.

One of the most pleasant surprises of learning about the wines of South America was to discover Pinot Noir alternatives that are really terrific. The best present a structural presence that I have not found in California, for example. There I have found thick fruit and overwhelming oak that many people like but that I find, well, offensive. Similar products from Australia and New Zealand led me to abandon Pinot Noir from anywhere but France.

No longer! Herein, the reader will find reviews of Pinot Noir that are treasures. The great advantage of a terrific Pinot Noir is that couples can enjoy them and find their favorites to share for special moments. As Aurelio Montes Junior explained, so many men who like big, full-bodied reds are frustrated that their women companions do not appreciate the same. A terrific Pinot Noir overcomes this problem. After this enlightenment, I have nicknamed great Pinot Noirs as "preludes to a kiss".

One of the essential ingredients to a terrific Pinot Noir is a long, cool growing season. The tropical climate of South America offers that in abundance. This allows a later harvest and fuller, more intense grapes. The result is a departure from what I had experienced in recent years. There are still the fruit bombs and the overly oaked versions, just like those of the other countries. After all, if they sell they will be imitated. The other end of the spectrum is equally bad. Tepid, watery, uninspiring mild efforts that try not to offend are common.

But the great winemakers know what to do with Pinot Noir when given the opportunity. The grape at its best is medium-bodied, with a round berry taste, supported by spices, and presented with a rich elegance in a balanced manner that allows the flavor to come through. Oaking should be minimal and subtle. See Montes, Loma Larga, Ventisquero, and Veramonte from Chile, among others. The fruit should be vibrant, the spices adding complexity. There is depth of flavor, but in a subtle, smooth presentation. Cherry themes frequently come to the forefront, the tannins are stealthy, the intensity is present but finessed.

In the reviews below, Chile clearly has developed the great Pinot Noir of this century. Although there are many attractive alternatives, four wineries stand out in my mind: Montes, Loma Larga, Ventisquero and Veramonte. Montes believes the best Pinot Noir comes from the Leyda Valley, the others from Casablanca Valley. Most have very reduced amounts of cases so they are not easy to find but some 75% is exported to the U.S. Trapiche, among others from Argentina, has a wonderful Broquel Pinot Noir, as well. In the upcoming years, the Pinot Noir produced by these South American wineries will make their mark internationally and reap the rich rewards that they merit.

WINE LABELING AND CLASSIFICATIONS

*E*ach country has its rules and regulations on wine classifications. Some countries are very strict, such as France.

Argentina and Chile enforce the following:

For a region to be listed on a label, at least 75 percent of wine in the bottle must originate there.

Hence, for the bottle to say that the wine is from Casablanca Valley, 75 percent of the wine must originate from that valley.

Internationally, however, the standard is 85 percent. Hence, South American exporters, which include all of the wineries reviewed in this book, adhere voluntarily to the 85 percent standard.

When a grape variety, for example, Cabernet Sauvignon, is listed on the label, at least 75 percent of the wine must come from the variety, in this case Cabernet Sauvignon.

Again, the international standard is 85 percent, so the Argentine and Chilean producers adhere to the standard of 85 percent in order to declare the wine a particular varietal.

When a vintage is listed on the label, at least 75 percent of the wine must be produced in that year.

As the standard once again, is 85 percent internationally, the Latin producers adhere to that same standard. Among some of the highest quality wines, if a vintage is not up to their standards for the brand in question, that year may be skipped, as Don Melchor. AlmaViva, and Altair, among others have done in bad years.

Declaring a wine a Reserva, Reserva Especial, Reserva Privada, Gran Reserva, or other similar description that indicates a higher than normal quality is a decision of the winery, but only may be done if the wine has a minimum of 12 percent alcohol, has "distinctive organoleptic properties," and finally, has had some oak treatment.

Organoleptic means "of or having certain sensory characteristics." Presumably, a Reserva is a wine with superior aspects, such as a deep aroma or a delicious taste that motivates the winemaker to place a distinctive label on it to distinguish that wine from the other wines. It should be noted that a Reserva usually has but does not HAVE to have been oaked. In order to use the other descriptions, Chilean law requires at least some oaking;

Finally, Argentine and Chilean law requires the alcohol content to be on the label and Chilean wine must have a minimum content of 11.5.

ANALYSIS AND CRITERIA

*T*he criteria for evaluating a wine used herein are divided into the following categories:

COLOR: The visual observation should be attractive and pleasurable. We should be invited to taste by what we observe. The color should not be weak and watery; it should be firm, even hard to define. If the color is complex, the wine is more likely to be as well.

AROMA: The word itself brings such pleasurable visions to mind. With only five letters, aroma has three syllables. It is a word that flows off one's lips. Aroma is the magic of flowers, that great indefinable characteristic of a woman, and most certainly, an essential aspect of a delicious wine.

Using wonderful grapes does not guarantee a great aroma. Smelling the wine should offer the observer a multitude of information. Will the wine be complex? Is it fully mature or does it need more time to develop? Has the barreling taken over the taste so one smells more wood than grape, and so forth.

Wine, like one's lover, reveals so much in the scent. The nose prepares one for the taste and is probably the second most important aspect of the rating after the taste itself. Aroma! It should be inviting and inspiring.

BODY: The concept of fullness – Does the wine have that hard-to-define feeling that the taste is complete? If the wine is big and bold in style, does it have a taste that reflects what it is all about or does it not fully complete its goal? If it is to be light and aromatic does it avoid being small and unobtrusive? The mouth, in other words, not the nose, will determine this criterion.

PALATE: As we taste the wine, do we feel the complexity it is supposed to offer as our senses are exposed to the full taste? Does it develop and have different levels? Does it reveal different levels of pleasure? Sensuality? Do we notice different aspects of the wine, fruits, terrain, minerals, smokiness or levity?

FINISH: Do we have a pleasurable fullness and consistency in its finish that makes us want to have more or does it leave a bitterness or unpleasantness that makes us say good riddance? Finish is a very important aspect of taste. as we should desire to repeat and continue the experience. With food, it should complement what we are eating. We should have a complete experience that a poor finish impedes.

Rating by numbers theoretically is the clearest way of telling the reader where the wine ranks. But wine tasting is not calculus or geometry. It is subjective to an extreme.

A number system indicates, per se, that somehow the evaluator is talented enough to objectify each wine and rate it so that one is clearly great, while another is fantastic without being great.

If everyone else does a numerical rating, who am I to be different? Well, I recognize my foibles – both the evaluator and the wine have good and bad days, good and bad mixtures and to be honest, if one has five terrific wines on five different days from five different bottles, blindly, and with no knowledge aforethought, it is extremely unlikely the numerical score will be the same each time.

Hence, a numerical score is inherently unfair to the wine and in my opinion should be in a category, not a number. For instance, is the wine great? Then its numerical score would be around 94 to 100. And so forth down the line.

Therefore the scoring used herein goes like this:

GREAT: The wine fulfills the best possible qualities in all categories, offering an absolutely wonderful, fully sensuous, arousing feeling and has nothing lacking.

OUTSTANDING: Similar to great but missing something. Still, a wonderful experience that we want to come back for – roughly, in the low 90s.

VERY GOOD: The positives outweigh the negatives by a large margin but it does not offer everything in all of the criteria, though it continues to be a predominantly positive experience and you would want to do it again.

GOOD: Low 80s; has a lot going for it but is not a fully positive experience. Frequently the finish is mediocre or the full taste of the grape does not come out. Something is missing but it is still an enjoyable wine, rarely mentioned herein.

INADEQUATE: I will not discuss inadequate wines in this book.

Argentina

Argentina

Argentina is known as the country of tango, soccer, Evita, and Maradona. With seemingly constant economic crises and accusations of political corruption, Argentina frequently is not considered a serious country. However, its premium wines are serious. Susana Balbo, the president of Wines of Argentina, feels she has a mission to alter the international image of the country by teaching people all over the world how great the top wines are that they produce.

Historically, Argentina, the fifth largest wine producing country in the world, makes and consumes unusually large amounts of inexpensive and unappealing wines. In the 1970s, Argentina had an average yield of 22 tons of wine per acre, whereas Bordeaux and Napa had an average of from two to five tons per acre.

The yield of wine land is inversely proportional to the quality of the wine produced. Today, the yield has decreased significantly with premium wine vineyard yields now comparable to the French. The times are changing in wine production in Argentina.

Argentina has 390,000 acres of planted vineyards, almost 3 percent of the world's plantations. Of that amount, Mendoza possesses 75 percent, with Patagonia to the South and Salta to the North being two other principal wine-producing areas. Since 1984 when Luigi Bosca, Catena and others began exporting some premium wines in small amounts, Argentina began to develop interesting wines. In the last decade or so, with numerous foreign investors and winemakers coming to Mendoza, for the most part, Argentina has made its entrance into the world market of premium wines.

The country's first vines were planted by Spanish conquistadors in 1554. In the following 300 years, the country's wines were grown mostly by missionaries. Argentina became independent from Spain in 1816. In 1852, a quantum leap was made with the inauguration of the country's first school of agriculture, Quinta Nacional, located in Mendoza. Founded by the French agronomist, Michel Aime Pouget, who introduced the important grapes to Mendoza, including Malbec clones from Bordeaux and Cahors, the institute continues to graduate agronomists, oenologists, and viticultural engineers, who lead the tremendous growth in the area.

Today, Argentina, a country of immigrants, mostly Eastern and Western Europeans, consumes 30 liters of wine per capita, as compared to only seven liters in the U.S. and 20 liters in Australia.

Like Chile and Australia, most of the wine consumed in Argentina is what used to be called grocery store or bulk wine and now is renamed carton wine, due to the tetra-pak system of preserving liquids such as milk in patented carton containers.

Unfortunately for the premium wines, there are still large amounts of inferior Malbecs being exported in bulk and inexperienced consumers have a misimpression that much of Malbec is not good. They forget the price they are paying is not sufficient for the quality wines. Nevertheless, one can buy fantastic wines, Malbec and other Argentine wines, under $15 in the U.S., and one of the purposes of this book is to show which ones are those quality wines.

Surprisingly, at least to this writer, Mendoza and most of Argentina is a desert. Mendoza has an average of eight inches of rain per annum. Its only water source is the run-off from the Andes. For over one hundred years, Argentina has had a very sophisticated and surprisingly organized irrigation system, which was fundamentally started by the original Indians and Incas. Today, the land that has real value consists of those plots with rights to water from this system.

Basically, the vineyards in the Mendoza area are oases in the midst of a desert. Nevertheless, most of Mendoza is between 1100 and almost 5000 feet above sea level. Salta vineyards, principally in the Cafayate Valley, go as high as almost 9000 feet.

As mentioned elsewhere herein, in parts of Mendoza where the architecture is inspired by the Indian and Incan cultures, it feels like we are in New Mexico, but at the feet of the Alps. It is a very unusual and surprising feeling, but it makes for a setting for planting wonderful grapes and producing wonderful wine.

Mendoza, as well as other parts of Argentina, has climatic advantages conducive to producing great wine. Although a desert, it receives a substantial supply of very pure water for controlled irrigation of the vineyards from the majestic Andes mountains. The high elevation eliminates most diseases and pests, as well as enabling a stronger amount of sun. There is little need for chemicals given these two factors.

The large swing between high daytime summer temperatures and cool nights allow for richer development of the grapes in the summertime. The colors are richer and the aromas stronger. Hang time for the deeper grapes like Malbec allows for ideal maturation, something that is not present for the same grapes in France's shorter season. The result of these climatic conditions is an environmentally friendly and sustainable viticulture.

Latitude of Mendoza is 33 to 35 degrees south of the equator and harvest takes place in the late fall, which is February to May. However, the average temperature is 59-66 degrees F, and there is little in extremes. The weather hazards are occasional hail, which is devastating when it occurs, forcing vineyards, in certain areas, to have netting over the vines, and Zonda, which are very hot, dry summer winds.

In the last decade, many wineries have acquired extremely sophisticated technology to measure the amount of water, sunlight, etc. taken in by the grapes on a daily basis, and have developed techniques to make leaves grow in such a manner as to shield the grapes from direct sunlight from 10:30 a.m. to 3 p.m.

New drip irrigation systems allow for more rational distribution of water, which is essential for premium wines. Protection against hail with protective mesh has all but eliminated this danger, which every few years would cause great damage.

These are just some examples of many techniques to improve the quality of the grapes. As a result, comparing the latest vintages to previous years may not be very useful since this knowledge and science was not available prior to 2001. The magnificent new wineries that are appearing in Mendoza are literally breaking new ground on so many fronts, scientific and oenological.

Malbec, unquestionably, is the most important grape in the country, with estimates of between 60 percent and 80 percent of the planted vineyards production. However, Argentina has some very "original" varieties that already are making distinguished wines and will make an impact on the international community to a greater extent in the near future.

Torrontes is the wine I have found to be quite original, becoming a delicious white wine as technology and planting techniques continue to improve. Similarly, Bonarda, originally from Europe a century ago, is a local red grape that has great blending results, and is becoming an important varietal on its own. Historically, Bonarda was the grape with the largest production as it is the base for much of the mass produced, inexpensive Argentina had previously been known for. Cabernet Sauvignon, Syrah, Chardonnay, Cabernet Sauvignon and Pinot Noir have Argentine producers with wines that can compete all over the world. We will examine in depth these extraordinary efforts herein.

One of Argentina's largest advantages in the export market is its low costs. Besides considerably lower wages for workers, there is the comparatively low cost of land.

At roughly $30,000 an acre, land costs one-tenth of that of Napa Valley. With crises seemingly cropping up annually in Argentina, many large international wine producers are hesitant to invest in such a complex economic environment. However, for those who have, the wonderful grapes grown in Mendoza, with original and fertile oasis terroir, and a university that is annually graduating talented agronomists anxious to produce wonderful wines, Argentina has a very bright future ahead in the premium quality wine categories.

FACTS ABOUT ARGENTINA

LOCATION: Bordered by the Atlantic Ocean to the East and the Andes and Chile to the West, in the Southernmost part of the Americas.

SIZE: Over 1 million square miles; 30 percent the size of Europe, it is the world's eighth-largest country

CAPITAL: Buenos Aires

POPULATION: 40 million, 98 percent of European descent, mostly Italian and Spanish

LANGUAGE: Spanish

RELIGION: Mostly Roman Catholic

CURRENCY: Argentine peso

ELECTRICITY: 220v with a three-pronged plug that needs a converter

Argentina is famous for the tango, great soccer and polo teams, and very special meats. The seasons are the reverse of the Northern Hemisphere, with harvest in the fall from mid February to April. The soil is alluvial with substrates of gravel, limestone and clay, resulting in most wines having strong hints of minerals. Argentina is the world's largest producer of grape concentrate.

Finally, it must be noted that in the medium to expensive wines, Argentina has many genial products. Most Icons, which is the name vineyards apply to their top of the line flagship wines, are around only $50, a range that competes with very good wines from California and Europe.

The few wines in the $100 areas are simply superb and are on par with wines two to three times that price. Here is a great chance to learn which wines are the great values of the world and on which levels for each group. We do not want to write about wines that are not enjoyable. In this section of the Argentine wines, the range is only from Very Good to Outstanding to Great. I did not like all the wines I tasted. But I only write about the ones I thought deserved this recognition.

ACHAVAL FERRER

Founded in 1998 by five friends, Achaval is today considered one of the premium wineries in Argentina. Located in various vineyards in Mendoza, Achaval has cultivated some very old vines into delicious red wines, centered around wonderful Malbec grapes.

Led by Italian winemaker Roberto Cipresso, the partners have attempted to make unfiltered, terroir-dominated, serious wines. 12,000 cases, 88% exported, U.S. largest destination.

There are three levels: The Malbec, Quimera, and finally, three single- vineyard Fincas. All are made with extremely low yield, hand-picked grapes. All require at least 40 minutes opened prior to drinking. www.achaval-ferrer.com

ACHAVAL FERRER MALBEC 2008

COLOR	Almost black fuchsia
AROMA	Big, round, elegant bouquet
BODY	Full, lots of grapes, muted mildly by oak; firm and round.
PALATE	Elegant and smooth; delicious berries, great follow through
FINISH	Smooth, delicious; must let breathe to fully appreciate

OUTSTANDING
100% Malbec, 10 Months in French oak, Boute barrels, $25

ACHAVAL FERRER QUIMERA 2007

COLOR	Intense violet
AROMA	Big, round, very inviting, sensual
BODY	Smooth, berry muted by oak, very round and even; delicious
PALATE	Big, lots of fruit; surprisingly elegant; dense and well structured
FINISH	Languishingly smooth, elegant, almost erotic; "Black Lace"

GREAT
38% Malbec, 24% Merlot, 24% Cabernet Sauvignon, 14% Cab. Franc. Super selected from very low yields, manual harvests, 1 year in French oak, 5,280 cases. Quimera means an impossible goal; in this case, perfection is what is trying to be achieved and it is very close! $40.

ACHAVAL FERRER FINCA MIRADOR 2007

COLOR   Intense violet
AROMA   Bouquet of berries and minerals, subtle
BODY   Very complex, feels very young; 2005 much more developed
PALATE   Very interesting and complex, lots of berries; 2005 similar
FINISH   Smooth, needs lots of aeration; 2005 marginally bigger, will age well

OUTSTANDING TO GREAT

Single vineyard, 100% Malbec wine; very complex and sophisticated, 2005 is marginally bigger in taste. Medrano section on the west bank of the Tunuyan River, ages very well, elevation 2400 feet, 13 acres of old vines (1921), extremely low yields, 15 months in new French oak Boute barrels. 1000 cases, $120

FINCA BELLAVISTA 2007

COLOR   Intense violet
AROMA   Round, but complex; inviting and smooth
BODY   Big, rich with lots of fruit, integrated oak tones. Very elegant
PALATE   Opulent, lots of fruit but very round and delicious; easy to drink
FINISH   Smooth, even, excellent; keeps on coming; wonderful

GREAT

Extremely low yield, hand picked, 100% Malbec. Unfiltered, no fining, single vineyard from Perdriel, vines aged from 1910, 15 months in new French oak. 753 cases, $120

ACHAVAL FERRER FINCA ALTAMIRA 2007

COLOR Purple, almost black

AROMA Very inviting and suggestive, round. 2002 deeper aroma and bigger

BODY Big with great berry, robust; 2002 bigger and smoother, fabulous

PALATE Velvety berry taste, round; 2002 silky smooth, very round

FINISH Smooth and elegant, terrific; 2002 same, only even better

GREAT

100% Malbec, La Consulta single vineyard, very serious. Ages extremely well. This one will keep improving. Should age at least 16 years with definite improvement each year $120

ALTA VISTA

Located in the posh suburb of Chacras de Coria, 20 minutes from downtown Mendoza, Alta Vista produces fabulous wines. Owned by the traditional French winemaking d'Aulan family, Alta Vista is based in a winery dating back to 1899. The company has preserved much of the old building and it is a magnificent tour de force, both for wine tourists and for cognoscenti.

Their store and tasting area is in part of the 1912 preserved area and should not be missed. Alta Vista owns 1200 hectares, between their land in Mendoza and Cafayate Valley. 220 Hectares are in production, mostly Malbec, which are located in some of the best areas of Mendoza, Vistaflores, Alto Agrelo, and Las Compuertas.

The d'Aulan group once owned Piper Heidsieck champagne, and still retains a percentage of Taittinger, as well as Chateau Dereszla, a classified vineyard in Tokay, Hungary. 140,000 cases, 50% exported.

Managed by the very knowledgeable Phillipe Rolet, Alta Vista is a jewel of French knowledge and style and fabulous tropical vines. Extremely tourist friendly with educational and fascinating tours, Alta Vista is wonderful stop for any visitor. www.altavistawines.com; altavista@altavistawines.com

ALTA VISTA CLASSIC TORRONTES 2007

COLOR   Pale Amber with tinges of green
AROMA   Inviting sweet bouquet of Citrus/Minerals
BODY   Full, smooth, delicious
PALATE   Some complexity, pleasingly tinge of
         sweetness, very smooth
FINISH   Delicious, refreshing, some complexity,
         slightly sweet; sensual

OUTSTANDING
100% Torrontes from Cafayete Valley A sensational entry level wine; $10.
This wine is written up here, along with Malbec and Rose, to emphasize
the extraordinary quality of this series of entry level, $10 wines. This winery
symbolizes the excellent match between French know how and the terroir and
micro-climates found in the desert of Mendoza.

ALTA VISTA PREMIUM TORRONTES 2008

COLOR   Yellow

AROMA   Inviting bouquet of muted grapefruit and minerals, Complex

BODY   Firm and refreshing; smooth somewhat complex, a big white wine

PALATE   Big taste of grapefruit with flowers; complex, extremely enjoyable

FINISH   Smooth citrus and flowers; long ending Terrific

GREAT

100% Torrontes; Just a perfect torrontes, fruity and smooth with lots of minerals; $14

ALTA VISTA PREMIUM CHARDONNAY 2008

COLOR   Yellow

AROMA   Semi sweet, inviting bouquet of Grapefruit and minerals

BODY   Less sweet than indicated by the nose, full, round taste

PALATE   Smooth, delicious, grapefruit dominance but not tart at all

FINISH   Refreshing and smooth

VERY GOOD

100% Chardonnay, 8 months in oak for 1/3, rest in tanks; 6000 cases, $14. Terrific buy

ALTA VISTA PREMIUM MALBEC 2007

COLOR   Intense Violet

AROMA   Round, Big Berry smell; Very inviting

BODY   Full, Firm, Structured but subtle berry taste

PALATE   Full taste of Malbec, very smooth; Round, dense

FINISH   Smooth, delicious yet subtly strong and structured; wonderful

OUTSTANDING TO GREAT

100% Malbec; 35,000 cases $14

ALTA VISTA ATEMPORAL 2007

COLOR   Intense Violet

AROMA   Enticing bouquet of dark berries with tones of minerals

BODY   Full Bordeaux style applied to great berries

PALATE   Smooth but strong; very sensual, structure and muted berries

FINISH   Smooth, trace of berries lasts and lasts Terrific

OUTSTANDING
45% Malbec, 35% Cab, 11% Syrah, 9% Petit Verdot; 1 year in oak. Atemporal means "timeless", $20

ALTA VISTA GRANDE RESERVE MALBEC 2006

COLOR   Intense Purple, Almost Black

AROMA   Berry bouquet with spices and minerals

BODY   Full, grapes abound muted by delicious oak

PALATE   Big, structured, but very smooth—great French touch

FINISH   Smooth, Sensual, Delicious

GREAT
100% Malbec very hard to beat; old vines from Uco Valley 15,000 cases, 1 year in French oak around $25

ALTA VISTA SERENADE SINGLE VINEYARD MALBEC 2007

COLOR   Very intense Violet

AROMA   Big bouquet of berries, very inviting and promising

BODY   Berries and minerals dominate this very big, structured delight

FINISH   Smooth, Sensual, Delicious BLACK LACE CORSET

GREAT
Seems impossible but this beats the other great malbecs—so big and strong, yet smooth. Truly great. Harmony between the hands of man and grapes of nature. ALTA VISTA SINGLE VINEYARD ALIZARINE AND TEMIS are equally fabulous, single vineyard Malbecs $55

ALTA VISTA ALTO 2006

COLOR   Black
AROMA   Muted Grapes, Very Full and inviting
BODY   Full, structured with unusual smoothness
PALATE Silky smooth, exotic tropical taste, Tres
        Francaise
FINISH Sensual and smooth; essence of great
        Argentine wine

GREAT
80% Malbec, 20% Cab; 18 months in new French oak, 18
months in bottles; 1100 cases 250 magnums Around $85

BODEGA ENRIQUE FOSTER/
BODEGA LORCA

Bodega Enrique Foster makes only Malbec wines, from an introductory version to an Icon. Mr. Foster lives in New York City and is a lawyer and businessman, originally from Spain.

His chief winemaker is Mauricio Lorca, who now makes wines under his own name in another vineyard, with Mr. Foster as his partner. They started selling wines in 2002. Both wineries are boutiques, with minimal production. The first vineyard purchased has vines planted in 1919. Foster makes 20,000 cases, half to U.S. Reservations required for visits www.enriquefoster.com; www.mauriciolorca.com

FOSTER IQUE 2008

COLOR   Deep purple
AROMA   Round, berry and mineral bouquet
BODY   Fruits and minerals in abundance; structured
PALATE   Smooth, intense, pure Malbec
FINISH   Smooth

VERY GOOD
Exports 80% of production, 100% Malbec; Ique is a popular nickname for Enrique in both Spanish and Portuguese.; $12

FOSTER RESERVE MALBEC 2006

COLOR   Deep violet
AROMA   Nice Bouquet of berries
BODY   Full; lots of berries and minerals, dense
PALATE   Smooth, delicious, will age well, very round
FINISH   Smooth, very easy for such a big wine, buttery

OUTSTANDING
100% Malbec, 1 year in French oak, 9 months bottled in cave, 3000 feet above sea level, 7000 cases; $23

FOSTER MALBEC LIMITED EDITION, 2005

COLOR   Deep purple
AROMA   Full and round, lots of berries and minerals
BODY   Big berry taste, smooth and delicious
PALATE   Smooth and round, minerals and berries,
          good structure
FINISH   Smooth, elegant, easy

OUTSTANDING
1200 cases; 100% Malbec, 15 months in new French oak,
should age well; $45

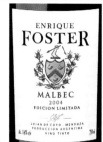

FOSTER FIRMADO 2006

COLOR   Intense violet
AROMA   Inviting round bouquet of big berries, mineral
          and spice   support
BODY   Smooth, full, delicious, firm
PALATE   Smooth, lots of berries and smoked spices;
          structured
FINISH   Smooth and elegant, very long and wonderful

GREAT
100% Malbec, only 350 cases, aged in new French oak 15
months; needs lots of time to breathe. Firmado means signed or signature; it's
intended to symbolize the quality the winery is striving for with its signature
wine. $90

MAURICIO LORCA GRAN OPALO BLEND 2006

COLOR   Deep purple
AROMA   Round, full berry bouquet
BODY   Strong, full, round, delicious
PALATE   Smooth, fruity, but very round
FINISH   Smooth, velvety

OUTSTANDING TO GREAT
No oak at all, 30% each Malbec/ Cab/Syrah, 10% Petit Verdot; only 400
cases. Terrific wine – this man knows what he is doing!! The vineyards have 1
hectare for each grape; planted 1999; $35

LORCA OPALO SYRAH 2006

COLOR   Deep purple
AROMA   Round, inviting, lots of berry bouquet
BODY   Full, round, smooth
PALATE Smooth, very even berry taste, good structure
FINISH Lots of berries, smooth and pleasing

OUTSTANDING
Uco Valley, no oak, 1000 cases, $18. The winemaker's
concept of not using oak is to offer a pure terroir that reflects the grape itself,
unaffected by wood or other factors that are not inherent to the grape. The
yield for these plantations are very low, concentrated, and of "great varietal
expression." I applaud this effort.

GRAN LORCA POETICO PETIT VERDOT 2007

COLOR   Deep purple
AROMA   Inviting and round
BODY   Full, smooth, berry infused, good structure
PALATE Smooth, full, easy to understand
FINISH Smooth

OUTSTANDING
100% Petit Verdot, 12 months in oak; $45

GRAN LORCA RESERVA 2007

COLOR   Deep violet
AROMA   Round and full, extremely inviting
BODY   Full, delicious, best of the group
PALATE Smooth with lots of berries and minerals, flowers all over
FINISH Smooth, delicious, long lasting end

GREAT
Aged in new French oak for 1 year, no filtration; 70% Malbec, 20% Syrah,
10% Petit Verdot. Terrific. 3000 feet above sea level; $45

BODEGA NORTON

Norton has a 115-year history and produces some of the best wines from the Mendoza region. Located in the premier region of Perdriel, some 25 minutes from downtown Mendoza, Norton has vineyards at altitudes from 2500 feet to over 3300 feet above sea level.

The winery produces 1,300,000 cases per annum, with 60% exported. Norton is a very traditional name in Argentina and in South America as a whole, so its local market sales are much more significant than most premium wineries. Pedro Minatelli is the talented head winemaker with a real passion for dedication to quality and preserving the terroir in each bottle.

Norton is extremely tourist friendly with tours every hour in both English and Spanish. There is a beautiful tasting room overlooking the vineyards and a very chic restaurant, open for lunch. The store is very accommodating.

Reservations: Turismo@norton.com.ar

NORTON TORRONTES 2009

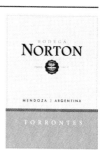

COLOR   Pale maize
AROMA   Inviting, calming citrus and mineral bouquet
BODY   Complex, very refreshing, clearly a serious wine
PALATE   Smooth, enjoyable mix of minerals and fruits
FINISH   Embedded citrus, long, enjoyable with wonderful mineral overtones

OUTSTANDING
100% Torrontes, terrific example of how Torrontes should taste, ideal for sushi. Very special and serious at only $10

NORTON SAUVIGNON BLANC 2009

COLOR   Very pale yellow
AROMA   Inviting with grapefruit and spices
BODY   Medium, refreshing, tropically fruited with added minerals
PALATE   Mild acidity, precise citrus tones, made for sushi and Cerviche
FINISH   Smooth, citric ending

VERY GOOD
100% Sauvignon Blanc, 33,000 cases. Norton owns 7% of Sauvignon vineyards in Argentina. Fermented and aged in stainless steel tanks; $10

NORTON MALBEC RESERVA 2006

COLOR   Intense violet
AROMA   Inviting berry bouquet
BODY   Big! Very balanced and round, berry and
         spices
PALATE   Complex taste of berries, spices, and minerals;
         smooth
FINISH   Round, smooth, long lasting

VERY GOOD
20,000 cases, 100% Malbec, $15

NORTON CABERNET SAUVIGNON RESERVA 2006

COLOR   Purple
AROMA   Round inviting cherry-like bouquet
BODY   Medium, smooth cherry/berry taste
PALATE   Easy to understand, some minerality with
         berry dominance
FINISH   Smooth, easy, ideal for a couple

VERY GOOD
Fermented and aged in oak for 1 year; 160,000 cases, $15; made for pork and
medium meats or grilled shrimp

NORTON PRIVADA 2006

COLOR   Intense fuchsia
AROMA   Very inviting, mild berry bouquet
BODY   Medium to full; smooth, blend of minerals,
         spices and cherry
PALATE   Lovely in the mouth, serious, terraces of fruits,
         great depth
FINISH   Elegant, with rolls of smooth-tasting berries

OUTSTANDING
40% Malbec, 30% of each Merlot/Cab. Originally made just for owners,
hence the name. Percentage of each grape fixed. Aged 16 months in new
French oak, $20

NORTON PRIVADA MALBEC 2006

COLOR   Intense violet
AROMA   Smooth bouquet of berries, very inviting
BODY   Firm, round, full. Terrific mix of berries, spices and minerals
PALATE   Smooth and delicious; Malbec standout, subtle oak influence
FINISH   Very round, languishing ending, rich

OUTSTANDING

First vintage, 16 months in new French oak, I year in bottle, 100% Malbec; part comes from 85-year-old vines, Agrelo vines 65 years old, $35

NORTON PERDRIEL 2005

COLOR   Intense purple
AROMA   Very inviting, complex mix
BODY   Very full, smooth and complex – Terrific
PALATE   Elegant and firm; smooth, mix of spices, minerals and   berries
FINISH   Sensual, elegant and great smooth ending

GREAT

60% Malbec, 28% Cab, 12% Merlot; single vineyard, 16 months in new French oak. Most serious and rewarding of all of Norton, $50.

GERNOT LANGES 2003

COLOR   Intense violet
AROMA   Very inviting, round notes of berries and minerals
BODY   Full, complex, great depth
PALATE   Sensual and complex with lots of berries and minerals
FINISH   Languishingly smooth, elegant; a special wine
GREAT

70% Malbec, 25% Cab, 5% Cab Franc; 16 months in new French oak, should age very well. Has the owner's name on it so it is the Icon of the group. $100

BODEGA SEPTIMA

Founded in 1999, with the purchase of 306 hectares in the prestigious Mendoza sub-section of Agrelo, Bodega Septima produces some very fine wines. Owned by the Spanish group Codorniu, famous in Spain for its Champagne style Cava, Septima has a modern winery, with superb architecture and a wonderful restaurant. The vineyards go right up the base of the Andes and the view from all over is spectacular. 100 hectares have been planted, almost all of which is some 3300 feet above sea level.

The winery was designed by architects from Mendoza and uses exclusively stones taken from the Septima property. Interestingly, the building of the winery used the "pirca" technique used by incan tribes to pile stones on top of each other to build walls for their residences. 80% of the wines are exported, with most going to the U.S. and Europe. Production is at 280,000 cases with capacity for 45% more. The winery has 1500 French oak barrels. Since 2000, Ruben Calvo, a Mendoza native and graduate of Colegio Don Bosco in his home town, has been the head winemaker for Septima.

With a modern tasting room and store, and an excellent restaurant, Septima makes for a fascinating visit. Septima is very tourist friendly but reservations are essential. www.bodegaseptima.com; spuchol@codorniu.com

BODEGA SEPTIMA CHARDONNAY 2008

COLOR	Pale Yellow
AROMA	Mild breeze of citrus and pear, very inviting
BODY	Subtle, complex layers of fruit and minerals, well-balanced
PALATE	Soft and delicious, very smooth, mild acidity, flowing fruits
FINISH	Long, sleek, smooth, Very refreshing, Elegant

OUTSTANDING

60% Chardonnay, 40% Semillon, no oak, very natural taste, outstanding value, $12

BODEGA SEPTIMA CABERNET SAUVIGNON 2007

COLOR   Violet
AROMA   Inviting subtle notes of red berries
BODY   Full, Well structured, mild oak tones
PALATE Round and smooth, layers of red berries, note
        of spices
FINISH Long, very pleasing,

VERY GOOD TO OUTSTANDING
100% Cabernet Sauvignon, 6 months in oak, $12

BODEGA SEPTIMA MALBEC 2007

COLOR   Deep Purple
AROMA   Bouquet of Big Red Currant Berries
BODY   Very Full and Masculine, Well-structured and
        Dense
PALATE Round, firm, Smooth with a big berry taste,
        spices/minerals
FINISH Long, rewarding, delicious

OUTSTANDING TO GREAT
100% Malbec, 6 months in oak, a remarkable value, $12

BODEGAS SEPTIMA GRAN RESERVA 2006

COLOR   Dark Purple
AROMA   Bouquet of dark currant berries
BODY   Full, Round, Complex berry flavors with
        minerals and spices
PALATE Dense grapes, pepper, spice tones, smooth,
        well structured
FINISH Long, persistent, delicious, Elegant

OUTSTANDING
55% Malbec, 32% Cabernet Sauvignon and the rest is Tannat, aged for 1 year
in new oak, $28

BODEGAS CARO

Bodegas Caro is a joint venture between Nicolas Catena (CA of Caro) and Baron de Rothschild (RO of Caro), the latter owning Lafitte Rothschild, one of the first growth Bordeaux classics.

The magnificent 125 year old winery is being carefully restored by the group and will be receiving tourists toward the end of 2010. Located within the confines of Mendoza city, Godoy Cruz sector, Caro produces 2 blends in a very French style, but with clearly some of the best Malbec produced in Argentina. Nicolas Catena has built a magnificent restaurant within the grounds of the winery, 1884, which is directed by Francis Mallmann, a distinguished Argentine master chef. Outdoor seating, open modern kitchen, beautiful bar and finishings, 1884, though expensive, is a do-not-miss gourmet location in the city of Mendoza.

Estela Perinetti is the outstanding General Director of Caro and created a magnificent pair of wines in what will be one of the most beautiful wineries in Mendoza. Born, bred and educated in Mendoza, Estela is a wonderfully knowledgeable winemaker and an objective source of information about Argentine wines. Visitors welcome with reservations www.lafitte.com; caro@lafitte.com

ALMANCAYA 2007

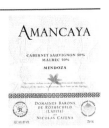

COLOR   Profound Violet

AROMA   Round, Smooth, Inviting, supple fruit; slight mineral bouquet

BODY   Full, Delicious Berries, Muted by Oak, round and smooth

PALATE   Fabulous, round and accessible, with delicate bursts of berries

FINISH   Long and smooth; keeps on going with velvet like finish

OUTSTANDING TO GREAT
Maybe the best buy in world for the price; 65% Malbec; 32% Cabernet Sauvignon, 2% Syrah. 22,000 cases. Mix varies annually depending on winemakers perception of best grape combination. Interesting fact: the first vintage was predominantly Cab; each year the amount of Malbec has grown and today it is the majority of the wine; 8 tons per hectare. $16

CARO 2006

COLOR   Deep Blackish Fuchsia

AROMA   Sensual and inviting with a round bouquet of berries

BODY   Very Full, but velvety smooth. Lasting flavor

PALATE   Fresh berries and minerals; Very smooth; French-like greatness

FINISH   Smooth and even; delicious; sensual, just wonderful

GREAT

Wonderful aging; the 2002 is superb and even more rewarding with a smoothness rare outside of France. The Argentine grapes make a perfect match for the French style. 2005 with similar qualities. Although not old enough to be sure, everything, indicates that CARO will age well for a minimum of 15 years, rewarding the patience with a superb, smoothness that gets better with the years. $50

CATENA ZAPATA

Nicolas Catena is the visionary leader of this family winery. With his children being the fourth generation to be actively involved in this magnificent venture, Nicolas, who is a former visiting professor at the University of California, was inspired by Robert Mondavi's wineries and his bravado in challenging the Bordeaux wines' prestige worldwide.

He felt Mendoza could do what Napa had done, and his family winery could do what Mondavi had done, and he set out to do it. Like many other wine lovers, I can vouch for Catena, in saying he has made wines that are world class and his vision and magnificent winery are true icons among great wines and great wineries.

The first generation Nicola planted his first vineyard in Mendoza in 1902. By 1963, Nicolas, now a PHD in economics, took over the family business, which at the time was a producer of popular bulk wine. By 1976, the Catena business was producing more than 20 million bottles of wine per annum, one of the world's largest. In 1983, Nicolas set down the vision to expand into premium wines. By 1991, he was exporting to the U.S. In 2000, his top wines were winning international blind tastings.

In 2001, the Agrelo winery was inaugurated and named Uxmal after the site of the Mayan ruins. Catena Zapata, in the shape of an actual Mayan temple located in Guatamala, is one of the most awe-inspiring in a city of magnificent wineries. Anyone visiting Mendoza absolutely must visit Catena Zapata, be it for the wine, be it for the architecture.

Catena Zapata is extremely tourist friendly and has a great wine tasting area and store. Reservations are recommended.

The Catena Zapata mid portfolio varietals, priced at $17, are all very good to outstanding. Its introductory Alamos varietals are good values, with special emphasis on the Chardonnay and Malbec that are the best of the group.
www.catenawines.com

CATENA ALTA CHARDONNAY 2007

COLOR   Maize with tinges of green
AROMA   Full, round with bouquet of muted grapefruit; extremely inviting
BODY   Complex with lots of citrus, minerals; full and very delicious
PALATE   Smooth, chewy, complex, elegant – CASHMERE and SILK
FINISH   Smooth and long lasting; ideal for sushi, fish, shrimp

GREAT
Single vineyard (Adrianna lot 1), 5000 feet above sea level, 100% Chardonnay, aged for 16 months in French oak, 60% new, $30

CATENA ALTA CABERNET SAUVIGNON 2005

COLOR   Purple
AROMA   Smooth with bouquet of berries
BODY   Medium; Burgundian with lots of berries and
        minerals
PALATE Smooth and pleasing; muted dark berry
FINISH Smooth and firm

OUTSTANDING
18 months in new French oak; 100% Cab, sourced from 3 vineyards; around
$35

CATENA ALTA MALBEC 2006

COLOR   Deep Violet
AROMA   Full bouquet of a berry mix; minerals and
        flowers
BODY   Full and smooth, develops as it aerates;
        Wonderful
PALATE Elegant and smooth; berry predominates;
        minerals/flowers blend
FINISH Smooth and elegant; delicious

OUTSTANDING TO GREAT
Sourced from 4 vineyards, aged for 18 months in new French oak; $39.
Please let aerate for 40 minutes.

NICOLAS CATENA ZAPATA 2006

COLOR   Intense purple
AROMA   Full and complex, extremely inviting
BODY   Big, complex; very smooth and delicious
PALATE Smooth, tasty, complex; clear taste of various
        grapes;sensual
FINISH Smooth like velvet; exceptionally long and
        delightful

GREAT
Blend of 60% Cab, 30% Malbec, 5% each of Petit Verdot/Cab Franc; 18
month in new French oak; single vineyard (Nicasia Lot 1) extremely low yield
$100

CHEVAL DES ANDES

The Argentine subsidiary of Cheval Blanc, Cheval des Andes is one of the premier winemakers of Argentina. Cheval Blanc was founded in Saint Emilion, France and is a first growth begun in 1832. Presently owned by Bernard Arnault and Baron Albert Frere, Cheval Blanc bought land in Lujon de Cuyo in the heart of Mendoza, first inaugurating Bodegas Chandon, where they produce champagne-like wine, and subsequently, Cheval des Andes, where the excellent "new world 'Grand Cru' is produced. "

Today, Cheval des Andes, which was created in 1999, in the magnificent sub-section of Vistalba, produces a Malbec-Cabernet Sauvignon blend that is a child of French winemaking talent with the fabulous terroir of Mendozan Malbec and Cabernet Sauvignon.

The wine is a product of an all-star cast of international names. Pierre Lurton is the French lead winemaker; the legendary Roberto de la Mota adds Argentine expertise. Nicolas Audebert is the talented and very charming winemaker for Cheval. He appears to be one of the main reasons Cheval is a successful mixture of the two cultures. He skillfully built a magnificent polo field in front of the beautiful structure that serves as the tasting room and cave for Cheval Blanc. One of the true gems I visited in Mendoza, the Cheval property is charming and luxuriously understated. Not normally open to the public, it is possible to visit with previous reservations.

Cheval varies its percentages of Malbec and Cabernet Sauvignon by having the winemakers of both Cheval and Terrazas blind test various combinations to select the wine that best reflects the terroir found in the grapes, with the French sophistication the winery is attempting to attain. 35 Hectares in Vistalba, 15 in Consulta.

I believe in time, this wine will be recognized as one of the great wines of the world. www.chevaldesandes.com

	2002	2006
COLOR	Intense Violet	Intense Violet
AROMA	Inviting bouquet of berries and minerals	More Berry bouquet than previous vintages, Delicious, Inviting, Sensuous
BODY	Full, very Complex, much Smoother, ages very well Structured	Subtle and complex, Malbec predominates, Dense and Delicious
PALATE	Full, Wonderfully Structured Great mix of berries and minerals	Full, Silky smooth, Elegant, will age well - is ready today
FINISH	Velverty smooth, Long, Delicate	Just about perfect

GREAT

5,000 Cases, 59% Malbec in most recent vintage, 39% Cab and 2% Petit Verdot; a total reversal from 2002 where Cab was 58%, Malbec 38%. 15,000 cases is the goal as grapes continue to improve; very low yield; must let breathe for 30 minutes at least, truly a superb wine. A true Grand Cru from Argentina, this effort places Cheval des Andes among the best wine in the world. Should be in any serious collection. $85

CLOS DE LOS SIETE

Clos de los Siete, meaning roughly, a group of seven, is a plan of Michel Rolland that today encompasses five wineries, each owned by different French entrepreneurs in a fabulous section of Uco Valley, Vista Flores, 110 kilometers South of Mendoza. The group contributes, in principle, 60% of its grapes to produce the wine Clos de los Siete. With the remaining wine, each partner has or will produce another wine(s) of their own label. Below are the results that the group has produced so far.

Michel Rolland is a successful and controversial wine consultant and now wine producer. His fame, basically, has been to apply certain of his principles to previously mediocre wineries, allowing them to make higher quality wines. So far as this project is concerned, he has helped make some terrific wines, which emphasize the terroir of the individual grape and the characteristics of the meso-climates of the region.

There are 850 hectares in total, of which 440 are planted. When all are fully operational, 70% of the grapes produced will be Malbec. Elevation is 3300 feet to almost 4000. The architecture of each project seems to be taken right out of the Indian heritage and oddly reminds one of New Mexico. Uco Valley is a desert oasis and feels like Santa Fe outskirts. Sitting in the winery, however, the magnificent view of the snow-capped Andes is reminiscent of the Alpes. The locale is a beautiful contrast of seemingly two different climates, but one that produces fabulous wines.

Reservations essential www.closdesiete.com.ar

CLOS DE LOS SIETE

COLOR	Very deep purple
AROMA	Round, fruity aroma, very inviting
BODY	Medium complexity; Malbec influence somewhat muted
PALATE	Smooth, berry and minerals dominate, Easy to understand
FINISH	Smooth, tasty, elegant

VERY GOOD TO OUTSTANDING
48% malbec, 28% Merlot, 12% Syrah, 12% Cabernet Sauvignon. Blend varies each year. 60% in oak 11 months; Quite French in style and should be very popular in a few years, this is only their 7rd vintage. A great buy at only $19

DIAMANDES GRAN RESERVA 2007

COLOR   Deep Purple
AROMA   Profound bouquet of berries, some spice Full
        and inviting
BODY   Full, A little on young side, very delicious; lots
        of berries/spices
PALATE   Terrific berry-spice blend; Opulent and dense
FINISH   Smooth, Very languid and long, Delicious

OUTSTANDING
70% Malbec, 30% Cabernet Sauvignon; a real star. 2006
much more mature and expect this vintage to grow with age; 17 months in
French oak; Owned by French wine group, Chateau Malartic-Lagraviere of
Bordeaux, $32

CUVELIER LOS ANDES COLECCION 2006

COLOR   Intense Violet
AROMA   Medium berries, opens slowly
BODY   Full, lots of berries; complex; should age well
PALATE   Round, firm berry taste; smooth, terrific right
        now
FINISH   Juicy and smooth as silk, wonderful; made for
        steak

OUTSTANDING
60% Malbec; 20% Cab, 10% Merlot, 5% each Syrah/Petit Verdot; 12 month
in French oak; style of wines "Bordeaux Grand Cru Classe". Limited yields.
A very serious wine, the first of three levels, Cuvelier is a project of Bertrand
and Guy Cuvelier, part owners of St. Julien's Chateau Leoville-Poyferre. $29

CUVELIER LOS ANDES GRAND VIN 2006

COLOR   Very Deep Purple
AROMA   Mild bouquet of Berries/minerals
BODY   Very Full, Round; delicious, Malbec muted by
        other grapes, oak
PALATE   Juicy, oaky, smoky, Big and Complex
FINISH   Smooth as silk Very French

GREAT
aged 15 months in 100% new oak; 70% Malbec, 10% each: Merlot/Cab/
Syrah Superb in every way. A fabulous wine, $50

CUVELIER LOS ANDES GRAND MALBEC 2006

COLOR   Black
AROMA   Fruity; very inviting
BODY   Full, lots of Fruit; Very Elegant
PALATE   Delicious; Round and Full; Great Malbec
             complexity
FINISH   Smooth, Long Very Smoky Berries

GREAT

100% Malbec; Icon of group; Will age very well. Spectacular!

FLECHA DE LOS ANDES GRAN CORTE 2005

COLOR   Intense Purple, almost Black
AROMA   Inviting Berry Bouquet
BODY   Medium Very Fruity—Malbec stands out; spices
             and minerals
PALATE   Concentrated Berries; Smooth and easy; spices
             clear
FINISH   Velvety smooth Silky Delicious

GREAT

70% Malbec, rest Cab and Syrah; 100% aged 15 months in New French
oak; owned by Benjamin Rothschild and Laurent Dassault; housed in a
magnificent building and project

VAL DE FLORES 2004

COLOR   Deep Purple, almost Black
AROMA   Great, inviting bouquet of complex berries/spices
BODY   Full; Opulent; Round, Well-structured
PALATE   Silky; distinctive spices/minerals complement berries; Complex
FINISH   Smooth, Velvety and very Masculine

GREAT

the best of a terrific group; 60% Malbec, 20% each Merlot/Syrah. Terrific and
serious wine, Will age fabulously for years but is delicious right now

CLUB TAPIZ

This interesting winery and tourist Mecca is located on an estate originally built in 1890. With many tours, a 7 room hotel, a restaurant, and some serious wines, Club Tapiz occupies a little over 10 hectares. In June, 2006, the hotel was declared a Historical and Architectural Heritage site. The vineyards are in the Uco Valley and Agrelo, next to the hotel. Owned by Fincas Patagonicas, the winery is technologically advanced and produces many interesting wines. Obviously, the Club is very tourist friendly and visitors and groups are welcome. Club Tapiz is a location very near Mendoza city that one can use as a base to see other vineyards. www.tapiz.com.ar; turismo@tapiz.com.ar

ZOLO TORRONTES 2009

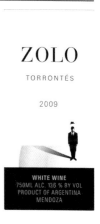

COLOR   Pale Maize
AROMA   Alluring bouquet of grapefruit and flowers
BODY   Full, complex, Muted Grapefruit, Tropical Flowers
PALATE   Elegant, sweet overtones, Needs lots of time to open up
FINISH   Very smooth, long,

OUTSTANDING
100% Torrontes, delicious wine after 30 minutes, some sweetness resembling Riesling but much more complex and interesting, $9

ZOLO CABERNET SAUVIGNON RESERVE 2006

COLOR   Intense Violet
AROMA   Smooth berry bouquet
BODY   Full, Round, Subtle
PALATE   Elegant, lots of Red and Black Berries
FINISH   Smooth, long, very enjoyable

OUTSTANDING
1 Year in oak, San Pablo Estate in Uco Valley, single vineyard, $12

ZOLO MALBEC RESERVE 2006

COLOR   Deep Purple
AROMA   Inviting bouquet of Cherry and dark berries
BODY   Full, dense, Layers of berries
PALATE   Expressive tones of minerals complement the
           berry power
FINISH   Big, long, well formed

OUTSTANDING
14 Months in new oak, $18

TAPIZ RESERVA SELECCION DE BARRICAS 2004

COLOR   Violet
AROMA   Subtle Whiff of Blackberries
BODY   Full, smooth, will reach peak in a few years
PALATE   Complex, many layers of fruit, Sensual
FINISH   Smooth, long, Vivid

OUTSTANDING
46% Cab, 38% Malbec, 16% Merlot, 16 months in French oak, Uco Valley,
Flagship of group, terrific $35

COLOME

Colome is one of the fascinating stories of Argentinean wines. Founded in the 1830's by the then Governor of Salta, located in the Northern mountains of Argentina, Colome has the highest elevation of any vineyard in the world, as well as being the oldest winery in the country. The founder's daughter brought over European vines in the mid 1850's, principally Cabernet Sauvignon and Malbec. Four hectares of these plantations are active today. Additionally, another 17 acres have vines between 80 and 120 years old Due to the high elevation, there are no disease issues and the winery is biodynamically organic, using organic compost in lieu of fertilizer.

In 2001, the winery was purchased by Hess family wines. With 96,000 acres, Hess intends to plant some 370 more acres, thereby doubling its present size. Located in the Calchaqui Valley, the land has been farmland for many centuries belonging first to the Calchaqui tribe and later by the Incans. The Spanish Conquistadors finally took the land from the Indians. The Hess family farms many agricultural products as well as animals, principally sheep, much like the Incans did hundreds of years ago. He also refurbished the 1831 winery with the most modern, state of the art equipment, which now enables the company to produce 1,300,000 bottles of wine! Some of the vines are planted at more than 9,000 feet above sea level in his second winery, Altura Maxima (highest elevation).

The winery has a small chic hotel, a gourmet restaurant, a church and is very tourist friendly, Reservations required Info@bodegacolome.com

COLOME TORRONTES 2008

COLOR	Lemon
AROMA	Enticing bouquet of citrus, whiffs of flowers
BODY	Layers of grapefruit, lemon, Gardenias, Full, Delicious
PALATE	Refreshing, Round, stylistically soft, mild acidity, Complex
FINISH	Smooth, long, very elegant

OUTSTANDING
100% Torrontes, not bubbly nor heavy; no bitterness, an ideal accompaniment for shrimp, sushi, Thai food. $12

COLOME MALBEC 2007

COLOR   Very Intense Purple

AROMA   Red berry, spices

BODY   Full, very well structured, with a firm density and balance

PALATE   Round and very intense, Delicious, big fruits and spices, Velvet

FINISH   Elegantly smooth, very long and languid; sensual to a fault

GREAT

100% Malbec,15 months in French oak, just terrific, $20

DOMAINE JEAN BOUSQUET

Jean Bousquet is a transplanted French winemaker who established his winery in Tupungato, Mendoza in 1997. Originally from Carcassonne, Jean was born into the third generation of a wine growing family. The vineyard is certified organic and intends to reflect the minerality of the soil. All of its wines are estate bottled, most single vineyard. With originally 265 acres of idyllic wine conditions, the vineyard is about 4000 feet above sea level and has a surprisingly significant production of over 150,000 cases, some 30% of which goes to the U.S. Visits with reservations are welcome. Jean Bousquet lives on the winery grounds.

Jean Bousquet has five introductory level, premium varietal wines that are very good. Chardonnay, Rose, Malbec, Merlot, and Cabernet Sauvignon. They sell on average for about $12. www.jeanbousquet.com.ar

DOM. JEAN BOUSQUET CHARDONNAY PINOT GRIS RESERVA 2008

COLOR   Yellow
AROMA   Tropical Citric fruits and minerals very inviting
BODY   Full, round, minerals, well balanced, Delicious and very smooth
PALATE Elegantly refreshing, Dense layers of fruit, great with fish
FINISH Smooth and round, languidly long and clean

OUTSTANDING
85% Chardonnay and 15% Pinot Gris, unoaked, 100% from vineyards in Tupungato, 4000 feet above sea level, $18

DOM. JEAN BOUSQUET PINOT NOIR RESERVA 2007

COLOR   Violet
AROMA   Wonderful Bouquet of Muted Red Fruit, very inviting
BODY   Medium, bold for a pinot; Elegant, French in style, well-balanced
PALATE Burgundy-like; Smooth delicious, great tropical fruit
FINISH Very smooth and elegant; French style married to tropical fruits

OUTSTANDING TO GREAT
100% pinot noir, 10 months in oak, 4 months in bottles, First vintage, single vineyard in Tupungato, 4000 feet above sea level, $18

DOM. JEAN BOUSQUET MERLOT RESERVA 2007

COLOR Dark Purple
AROMA Very inviting, Complex mix of Red berry with
       spicy overtones
BODY   Medium, round, smooth, Beautiful fruits, oak
       finish
PALATE Opulent, Dense diverse fruit, oak overtones
FINISH Long, Easy, Delicious,

OUTSTANDING
90% Merlot, 10% Malbec, Single vineyard, 4000' above sea level, 10 months in
French oak, 4 months in bottle, $18

DOM. JEAN BOUSQUET MALBEC RESERVA 2007

COLOR Dark Purple
AROMA Very inviting, Lots of berries, spicy notes,
       French touch
BODY   Round and complex, lots of fruit, well-
       balanced, Delicious
PALATE Dense, Supple, Elegant but very masculine,
       Fruits are just right
FINISH Smooth and long;

OUTSTANDING TO GREAT
85% Malbec, 5% each: Syrah, Cabernet Sauvignon, Merlot. 10,000 cases, 10
months in Oak, 4000' above sea level, $22.

DOM. JEAN BOUSQUET CABERNET SAUVIGNON RESERVA 2007

COLOR Dark Purple
AROMA Full body, almost smoky; lots of fruit; very
       inviting
BODY   Full, Very Bordeaux-like, Layers of fruit,
       Well-structured
PALATE Tones of black currant; diverse minerals,
       Delicious; Muted Fruit
FINISH Smooth Elegant Velvety

GREAT
85% Cabernet Sauvignon 15% Malbec 10 months in oak; 2000 cases, Great
Terroir, mixture of French know-how and style with great tropical grapes. An
artist's production, $20

DOM. JEAN BOUSQUET CHARDONNAY GRANDE RESERVE 2008

COLOR   Maize
AROMA   Chablis like, Inviting; Wonderful bouquet
         of Tropical fruits
BODY   Full and complex; lots of minerals,
         Delicious
PALATE   Silky, layers of apple, pears, great minerality; Burgundian, elegant
FINISH   Subtle, smooth and delicious, lingering ending, a real treat
GREAT
100% Chardonnay 1 year in oak, 14 Months in Bottle, 1000 cases, single
vineyard, 4000 feet above sea level, Price $30

DOM. JEAN BOUSQUET MALBEC GRANDE RESERVE 2006

COLOR   Black
AROMA   Very round, inviting, Complex
BODY   Full, Layers of Fruits and spices, Complex;
         Bordeaux like
PALATE   Elegant and smooth; great blend of minerals
         and spices/fruits
FINISH   Long, Smooth, Superb,
GREAT
Truly emblematic of talent and dedication, 85% malbec 5% each of Cabernet
Sauvignon, Merlot, Syrah Flagship of the winery, single vineyard, 1 year in
French oak, 1 year in bottle, Fabulous French style with special grapes, $30

DOM. JEAN BOUSQUET MALBEC DULCE 2008

COLOR   Dark violet
AROMA   Smooth sweet fruit, Very intense and rich
BODY   Round, Full, elegant, sweet, great with
         chocolate
PALATE   Smooth, sweet, but not over-powering
FINISH   Great way to end meal; smooth and delicious
GREAT
100% Malbec, 1 year in oak, 8 months in bottle, Single vineyard, 4000' above
sea level, $16

DOMINIO DEL PLATA

Founded in 2001, with state of the art technology, in Agrelo, Mendoza, this winery is the creation of Susana Balbo. With a beautiful building in the midst of 21 hectares, the winery and residence found life in the micro-climate of Lujan de Cuyo. This winery is known for its dedication to detail and its eco-protective culture.

Susana is well known in the Mendoza area for her knowledge and dedication to her art. With a rich curriculum dating back to 1981, she is an ambassador for the talent and serious dedication all of the winemakers in Argentina possess. She represents the forward looking, serious generation that is present in Argentina today.

Total production 200,000 cases across the 4 outstanding brands described below, 100% export, 70% to the U.S. Dominio Del Plata has been awarded the ISO 22000 certification for its food safety management system. The winery is also a leader in using sustainable farming and socially responsible initiatives. Tourists with previous reservations are welcome. www.dominiodelplata.com.ar

CRIOS TORRONTES 2009

COLOR   Pale Yellow
AROMA   Citrus and minerals dominate a very inviting bouquet
BODY   Medium, lots of muted fruit, must be drunk young
PALATE   Very refreshing, somewhat complex: lemon, flowers, minerals
FINISH   Smooth and long lasting

OUTSTANDING
Crios means "offspring" and Susana feels that her wines are her children; Torrontes is from Cafayate Valley, near Salta on vines some 31 years old. Susan Balbo has planted Torrontes grapes in Mendoza and expects to produce Torrontes from this vineyard in the coming years. $15

CRIOS CHARDONNAY 2008

COLOR   Pale Yellow with tinges of green
AROMA   Round and inviting, touch of oak
BODY   Medium with a certain complexity
PALATE   Smooth, light, easy to drink
FINISH   Touches of citrus, smooth, a little smoky adding to the complexity

VERY GOOD
100% Chardonnay, refreshing, $15

CRIOS SYRAH BONARDA 2007

COLOR Deep Purple
AROMA Inviting with tones of berries and minerals, raspberry
BODY Full, Round, elegant, well structured,
PALATE Muted by oak, very smooth and round. Delicious
FINISH Elegant and very smooth long lasting

GREAT
50% each Bonarda/Syrah Very elegant and original The best Crios for my taste; 11 months in oak, Agrelo and Uco valleys. $15

BENMARCO CABERNET SAUVIGNON 2007

COLOR Violet
AROMA Round with lots of berries
BODY Round and Fruity, tinges of minerals and smoky spices
PALATE Very even and fruity smooth to the taste
FINISH Smooth and lingering

VERY GOOD
85% Cab, 10% Merlot, 5% Cab Franc. 11 months in oak, $20

BEN MARCO MALBEC 2007

COLOR Intense Violet
AROMA Round beautiful bouquet of berries, muted-enhanced by oak
BODY Full, Complex and enjoyable, Round taste of berries and spices
PALATE Complex feel of berries, spices, minerals; dense, delicious
FINISH Smooth wonderful mix of flavors, long lasting

OUTSTANDING
90% Malbec with 10% Bonarda, which works perfectly. 34,000 cases. Great deal at $20

BENMARCO EXPRESIVO 2006

COLOR   Intense Violet
AROMA Very inviting complex mix of berry bouquet
BODY   Full, very round and delicious, Malbec mix of
         berries
PALATE Rewarding, Complex, Interesting, Great Balance
FINISH   Smooth, very subtle, LONG GOLD
         EARRINGS

GREAT
60% Malbec, 10% each of Syrah/Cab/Tannat/Petit Verdot.
Very creative and delicious. Rewarding to consumer; only 1500 cases $35

SUSANA BALBO CABERNET SAUVIGNON 2006

COLOR   Deep Violet
AROMA Very inviting bouquet of berries and minerals
BODY   Medium to Full
PALATE Round, terrific, Fruit, berries, Minerals,
         Smooth
FINISH   Smooth, Muted tones of fruit

OUTSTANDING
85% Cabernet Sauvignon, 15% Merlot, 80% in new French oak, 13 months.
$25

SUSANA BALBO MALBEC 2007

COLOR   Intense Violet
AROMA Inviting bouquet of berries and minerals,
         muted by oak
BODY   Full round taste of Malbec worked in oak to
         almost perfection
PALATE Smooth, full bodied, Round taste of berries,
         heightened by spices
FINISH   Smooth, elegant, long lasting

OUTSTANDING TO GREAT
90% Malbec, 10% Cab, 11 months in oak, 3300 feet above sea level, single
vineyard, Agrelo, a terrific wine –great buy! $25

SUSANA BALBO BRIOSO 2005

COLOR   Intense Purple, almost black
AROMA   Very inviting bouquet of layers of berries
BODY   Full, Bordeaux-like blend of 5 grapes, Well-
        structured
PALATE Round, dense, incredibly smooth
FINISH Elegant, silky smooth, languid, special: SILK
        STOCKINGS

GREAT

An icon of the winery, 65% Cab, 10% Cab Franc,
15% Malbec, 5% Each Petit Verdot/Merlot; unfined,
unfiltered (like all of Dominio del Plata wines), 500 cases, Blind taste this
against top level Bordeaux. The 2001 is still delicious and very complex; took
forever to open up (over 40 minutes) but rewarded this taster with great spice
and mineral complements to the dark, intense berry. This is a very serious,
delicious wine $45

NOSOTROS 2006

COLOR   Intense Violet
AROMA   Inviting bouquet of Dark Berries, Spices and
        Minerals
BODY   Full and Round; Terrific right out of the bottle,
        Keeps growing
PALATE Very Smooth but with great personality;
        Wonderful berries, Spices
FINISH Like silk burgundy; languishingly wonderful

GREAT

100% Malbec, 2nd vintage, just superb, surprisingly delicious as soon as it
is opened and just keeps getting better as it airs; 40 year old vines. This is
another very serious wine with minimal production.$100

DONA PAULA

The Argentinean subsidiary of the Chilean Claro Wine Group and sister of the outstanding Santa Rita Winery, Dona Paula has achieved a prominence of its own, beginning with its excellent introductory varietals in its Los Cardos line, through to the top of the line Seleccion de Bodega.

The first investment was in 1997 with the acquisition of 80 hectares of Malbec and Chardonnay vineyards in Finca el Alto in Lujan. The following year the Los Cerezos Estate inTupungato was purchased. Another two estates were purchased 5 years after. Today, located in the Lujan de Cuyo section of Mendoza, Dona Paula produces over 300,000 cases of wine, of which 125,000 is exported to the U.S.

Most of its vineyards are at 3300 feet above sea level. The winery opened in 1999. Today, over 54 countries import the Dona Paula line of wines. Edgardo del Popolo is the team leader for the vineyard and is an expert in the selection of vineyards and their particular grapes. Together with David Bonomi, a talented, young winemaker, he has developed terrific wines at very fair prices, which is finding great reception all over the world. Under his leadership, the winery has over 730 hectares today, 5 times the original purchase. He accurately represents the passion his team has for what they do! Reservations for visits are required. www.donapaula.com.ar; info@donapaula.com.ar

DONA PAULA ESTATE SAUVIGNON BLANC 2009

COLOR   Pale Yellow
AROMA   Muted Citrus tones
BODY   A certain complexity with floral notes over citrus and minerals
PALATE   A wonderful reflection of the terroir; refreshing, delicious
FINISH   Smooth, velvety, Very refreshing

OUTSTANDING
From Tupungato, Uco Valley sector of Mendoza, $15

DONA PAULA VIOGNIER NAKED PULP 2008

COLOR   Maize
AROMA   Mild Citrus, very inviting
BODY   Round, slightly sweet, delicious, embedded citrus, Balanced
PALATE   Refreshing, nice sucrosity, Complex, opulent
FINISH   Smooth, compliments sushi and grilled fish

OUTSTANDING
from the excellent sand-rock soil of Vista Flores, at the foot of the Andes 3300 feet of elevation, 8 months in new French Oak $19

DONA PAULA ESTATE TORRONTES 2009

COLOR   Pale yellow
AROMA   Flowery, citrus bouquet
BODY   Citrus, minerals, flowers; lemon, with a slight
        sweetness
PALATE Complex mix, very interesting, refreshing
FINISH A sweet/sour mix, long in the taste; Ideal for thai and Japanese
VERY GOOD
1st vintage, new to US could substitute Riesling as it is much more interesting.
From Cafayate Valley near Salta in North 5600 feet above sea level, $14

DONA PAULA ESTATE MERLOT 2004

COLOR   Purple
AROMA   Complex, tones of black berries, inviting
BODY   Medium, round, Smooth
PALATE Ample, smooth, Dark berries abound; mineral
        overtones
FINISH Easy, Smooth, like a loose cashmere sweater

OUTSTANDING
single vineyard, 100% merlot, $16

DONA PAULA ESTATE CABERNET SAUVIGNON 2008

COLOR   Deep Purple
AROMA   Profound bouquet of black fruit and minerals
BODY   Smooth with a medium round taste of
        complex fruits Interesting
PALATE Spices and minerals compliment the Smooth
        Berries
FINISH Velvety smooth, long finish
OUTSTANDING TO GREAT
Cab 100%, 12 months of oak, French clones, Great value Uses sustainable
Agricultural Practices as all of the estate does, $16

DONA PAULA ESTATE MALBEC 2008

COLOR — Very Deep Violet

AROMA — Full bouquet of berries; Smooth and inviting

BODY — Full and round; Lots of Fruit, quite muted with oak

PALATE — Elegant Berry fruits, Very smooth

FINISH — Long and Velvety, Smooth

OUTSTANDING TO GREAT

100% Malbec, needs a little aging to be great; the 2006 is great. More complexity, deeper aromas, smoother. Was 2 months more in oak and it shows. Developed very well in the bottle; Great value, 20,000 cases. The 1999 version is fabulous and got much better with age, especially considering the improvements since that first vintage, in choosing grapes, as well as processing them.; $16

DONA PAULA SELECCION MALBEC 2006

COLOR — Black

AROMA — Full, Extremely inviting with muted grape bouquet

BODY — Fantastic, Very full and round Great Complexity; balanced

PALATE — Smooth Delicious, sensual Lots of Berries and minerals, well- structured

FINISH — Smooth, Great Malbec; Like black lace sensual

GREAT

100% Malbec, Tasted 2005, 2002, and 1999 (first vintage) The wine gets smooth and more delicious with age, the 2002 being the best of the group. Fabulous result of a natural, tropical Malbec grape, $50

FABRE MONTMAYOU

Herve Joyaux Fabre, originally from Bordeaux, purchased some outstanding vineyards in the mid 1990's and established his winery using Malbec vines that dated back as far as 1908. Based in Vistalba and surrounded by its original vineyards, the winery carefully hand selects the grapes it will use. Along with his vineyards in Patagonia, the company sells some 110,000 cases per annum. Visits require reservations. www.domainevistalba.com.ar

FABRE MONTMAYOU TORRONTES RESERVA 2009

COLOR   Very pale yellow
AROMA   Citrus, smooth and inviting
BODY   Somewhat complex, Medium, Lots of citrus
PALATE   Smooth and Round with lots of flavor Very refreshing
FINISH   Smooth; muted for a torrontes,
VERY GOOD
100% Torrontes, 9000 cases, excellent for Thai food, $12

FABRE MONTMAYOU BARREL SELECTION MALBEC 2008

COLOR   Deep Purple
AROMA   Inviting berry bouquet
BODY   Complex, lots of berries, dense
PALATE   Needs time to open, Smooth, complex, interesting
FINISH   Smooth, lots of berries
VERY GOOD
100% Malbec from 30 year old vines in Patagonia, 60% aged in French oak for 1 year; interesting as Patagonia grapes grow at sea level near beach in the Northern part of Patagonia. Should further improve with age. 2nd vintage, 20,000 cases, $15

FABRE MONTMAYOU GRAN RESERVA CABERNET SAUVIGNON 2008

COLOR   Deep Purple
AROMA   Intense bouquet of Berries/minerals; Very inviting
BODY   Big, Round, flush with red berries, Complex, Elegant
PALATE   Smooth, lots of tropical fruits and French styling; mineral laden
FINISH   Smooth, Delicious

OUTSTANDING
2500 Cases, 100% in French oak for 1 year, 100% Cab; $20

FABRE MONTMAYOU GRAN RESERVA MALBEC 2008

COLOR   Deep Purple, almost Black
AROMA   Smooth inviting, suggestive bouquet
BODY   Big, round, tasty, very elegant
PALATE   Complex, interesting berry, spice, mineral , masculine
FINISH   Smooth, Velvety Great with a steak

OUTSTANDING
100% in French oak for 1 year, 100% Malbec, from Vistalba, very serious and elegant wine, 9000 cases, 1st vintage in 2002, $20

FABRE MONTMAYOU GRAND VIN 2006

COLOR   Intense Violet
AROMA   Mixed Berries, very inviting
BODY   Full, Complex, Minerals and spices with Berries
PALATE   Very sensuous, oak mutes grapes; very smooth
FINISH   Very rewarding, smooth, delicious

OUTSTANDING
85% Malbec, 10% Cab, 5% Merlot; 100% aged in French oak for 16 months; Serious wine will age for a decade at least, $40

FAMILIA ZUCCARDI

The Zuccardi winery in Mendoza is perhaps the most important tourist center in the region. From an air balloon to wine classes, the tourist is presented with a plethora of educational and fun alternatives within the 175 hectares that the family owns in the Maipu sector of Mendoza. Blessed with vineyards in some of the best sections, Zuccardi has a rich family history. Over 4 decades ago, the family planted the largest vineyard for tempranillo in Argentina, in Santa Rosa, where today they have 375 hectares. In Uco Valley, there are 150 hectares of Malbec vineyards where the top of the line Zuccardi wines originate. Recently, the design of the bottles has been modernized and the emphasis made on the upscale wine alternatives that Zuccardi offers. Founded in 1963, it is family run with Jose Alberto Zuccardi directing, his son Sebastian in charge of viticulture, and winemaker Ruben Ruffo in charge of the Zuccardi lead wines. Rodolfo Montenegro creates the Santa Julia production The wines tasted herein have only been produced since 1997, less than a decade in some cases. They have evolved greatly since their inception. The entire estate runs under sustainable agricultural principles, with almost half the vineyards being certified organic. The company is very creative with their Vida Organica brand being exclusive for Whole Food stores. Their introductory Santa Julia line gives value for a low price and is readily available in the U.S. See their website for tours and reservations. Their family restaurant is a terrific lunchtime option. www.familiazuccardi.com

FAMILIA ZUCCARDI Q CHARDONNAY 2007

COLOR	Maize
AROMA	Inviting bouquet of pears and citrus
BODY	Medium thrust of sweet and citrus fruits muted by oak overtones
PALATE	Brisk and refreshing; nicely structured and an easy taste
FINISH	Long and crisp

VERY GOOD TO OUTSTANDING
100% Chardonnay, 6 months in French oak, $18

FAMILIA ZUCCARDI Q TEMPRANILLO 2005

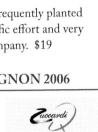

COLOR   Violet
AROMA   Subtle bouquet of red berries and mineral
         notes
BODY   Medium but unusually well-balanced
PALATE   Round and very pleasing; easy to understand.
FINISH   Long and smooth. Elegant

OUTSTANDING
100% Tempranillo, 1 year in American oak. This is an infrequently planted grape in Argentina, native to Spain. This version is a terrific effort and very original. Perhaps it is the best Q and best wine of the company. $19

FAMILIA ZUCCARDI Q CABERNET SAUVIGNON 2006

COLOR   Purple
AROMA   Mild bouquet of red berries
BODY   Medium, Layers of Red Berries, with mild
         spice/mineral support
PALATE   Round and Smooth with balanced structure
FINISH   Long, silky, lots of berries

OUTSTANDING
100% Cab, 1 year in new French oak, $19

FAMILIA ZUCCARDI Q MALBEC 2007

COLOR   Deep Purple
AROMA   Mild touches of dark currants and granite
         notes
BODY   Medium, Some structure, dense
PALATE   Round, easy, straightforward, not complex
FINISH   Persistent, evolving

VERY GOOD TO OUTSTANDING
100% Malbec from 2 estate vineyards, 1 year in French medium toasted oak barrels, $19

FAMILIA ZUCCARDI ZETA 2005

COLOR   Dark Violet
AROMA   Bouquet of dark fruits accented with spice
BODY   Full, dense, Waves of dark fruit; balanced
PALATE Round, combination of berry, minerals and
        spice
FINISH Long and deep

ZUCCARDI
ZETA
2005
MENDOZA · ARGENTINA

OUTSTANDING

2/3 Malbec, 1/3 Tempranillo, blend has a slight variation
year to year; Lots aged separately with Malbec in new
French oak for 1 year and Tempranillo 14 months in new
American oak barrels; when blended they age in bottles
for another 2 years; $49

MALAMADO MALBEC 2005

COLOR   Purple
AROMA   Enticing bouquet of an assortment of fruits and
        nuts
BODY   Full and complex; a real treat of tempered
        sweetness
PALATE Dense, elegant and rich; cleansing and delicious
FINISH Long and sensuous; great finish to a wonderful
        meal

MALBEC
FAMILIA ZUCCARDI

OUTSTANDING

100% Malbec, Very original Port-like wine with surprising
high quality and elegance; 10 days of classic fermentation
and treatment until a level of residual sugar of 120 grams per
liter; the wine is then fortified with wine alcohol and aged
in French oak barrels for 25 months! Result: 19.5% alcohol
content and a subtle after dinner mildly sweet wine. Superb
and original, $25

FINCA DECERO

Decero wines (decero means "from zero" or "from scratch") are serious, single vineyard wines produced from the Remolinos Vineyard at Finca Decero, a magnificent, modern hacienda-style winery in the Agrelo sub-section of Mendoza.

Remolinos means whirlwinds or mini tornados. If you sit on the deck of the Winery for a few hours, you will see little whirlwinds pop up over the countryside. Led by Juan Marco, general manager, and Marcos Fernandez, winemaker, Decero has just begun to be heard in the wine world for truly fabulous wines. Both gentlemen are talented, serious and dedicated to make the best quality product, without compromise. Their first vintage was 2006.

Located at the foot of the Andes, Decero is passionate about hand-selecting the best grapes from great vineyards and producing great wines. They have a magnificent restaurant and store, with panoramic views of the vineyards and the snow capped mountains. Decero is a class act: Beautiful, very functional, great wines; with a magnificent restaurant that should be on every serious wine tour of Mendoza; Beautiful store; breath-taking views, perfect in every way, especially with their artistic and delicious wines. Total production: 30,000 cases.

Visitors and tours welcome with previous reservations. decero@decero.com

DECERO MALBEC REMOLINOS VINEYARD 2007

COLOR   Intense Violet, almost black
AROMA   Deep, round Malbec bouquet very inviting
BODY   Full, complex Smooth; Well-balanced, delicious
PALATE   Elegant to a fault, Great taste, Big with lots of
         berries
FINISH   Smooth Elegant Long lasting TIGHT CASHMERE

GREAT
An example of how a Malbec should taste. 8,000 cases, Must breathe for 40 minutes. 16 months in French oak. $20

DECERO SYRAH REMOLINOS VINEYARD 2007

COLOR   Intense Violet
AROMA   Subtle inviting hints of dark fruit; Elegant in
         Bouquet
BODY   Medium to full Opulent. Structured.
PALATE   Medium complexity. Smooth with a berry taste
FINISH   Smooth as silk. Very elegant

OUTSTANDING
only 1000 cases, 16 months in French oak, $20

DECERO CABERNET SAUVIGNON REMOLINOS VINEYARD 2007

COLOR | Violet
AROMA | Round and Full; lots of berries. Very attractive
BODY | Full, complex, flush with dark berries. Very smooth
PALATE | Truly delicious and smooth Elegant Great Cab
FINISH | Smooth like velvet and black lace; Lingers happily

GREAT
16 months in French Oak, 5000 cases, $20

DECERO MINI EDICIONES PETIT VERDOT REMOLINOS VINEYARD 2006

COLOR | Intense Violet almost black
AROMA | Bold, Smooth and very inviting
BODY | Full, lots of Blueberries, muted by oak Very smooth
PALATE | Delicious and subtle; Smooth blend of berries
FINISH | Very Original, intense, smooth, elegant

GREAT
only 600 cases, 16 months in French Oak, 50% new. Normally a grape for blending, Petit Verdot is becoming a wine grape to stand on its own for sophisticated and capable winemakers, such as Decero's Marcos Fernandez, $35

DECERO AMANO REMOLINOS VINEYARD 2006

COLOR | Intense Violet
AROMA | Enticing notes of Flowers and Red Currant
BODY | Very intense but smooth. Full and complex; Dense,
PALATE | Big, Elegant; intense; mineral laden; Lots of berries, muted by oak
FINISH | Smooth, Delicious, Elegant and long lasting

GREAT
Icon; 60% Malbec, 35% Cabernet Sauvignon, 5% Petit Verdot. First vintage. 2007 not yet bottled but tasted from barrel and it is superb, probably even better than the great 2006. 22 months in new French Oak. Price around $55

KAIKEN

Kaiken signify wild geese that fly around Patagonia. The winery is the child of the Montes group of Chile and is based on some of the oldest vineyards in Mendoza. Beginning with their first vintage in 2002, Kaiken has acquired two significant vineyards in Agrelo (70 hectares) and Vistalba. Their wines are among some of the biggest reds in Mendoza, focusing especially on Malbec and Cabernet Sauvignon. The wines have been exported to 30 countries. Reservations are necessary for visits. info@kaikenwines.com

KAIKEN RESERVA MALBEC 2008

COLOR   Deep Violet
AROMA   Enticing bouquet of red fruit
BODY   Full, very big, Intense
PALATE   Well structured, Round, Dense, with
         smoky oak notes
FINISH   Smooth, very long, delicious

OUTSTANDING
5% Cab, rest Malbec, 60% aged in French oak for 8 months; $12

KAIKEN RESERVA CABERNET SAUVIGNON 2007

COLOR   Violet
AROMA   Alluring bouquet of red fruits
BODY   Full, very round, structured
PALATE   Layers of fruit, some complexity,
         Dense
FINISH   Smooth, long, Easy

OUTSTANDING
96% Cab, 4% Malbec, 8 months in American oak, $12

KAIKEN ULTRA MALBEC 2007

COLOR   Intense Violet
AROMA   Red Berries predominate, very inviting
BODY   Full, Big, Dense, well structured, balanced
         tannins, Elegant
PALATE   Very Round, layers of red berries/cherries,
         Silky smooth
FINISH   Long, smooth, Delicious

OUTSTANDING TO GREAT
100% Malbec, 1 year in French oak for 80% of the wine, $19.

KAIKEN ULTRA CABERNET SAUVIGNON 2007

COLOR   Dark Violet
AROMA   Black currant whiffs, very inviting
BODY   Full, Very direct, dense
PALATE   Easy to understand, Round, Lots of Fruit
FINISH   Smooth, Long,

OUTSTANDING

Cab 95%, 5% Carmenere, 1 year in French Oak, from 50 year old vines, $19

LUIGI BOSCA

Luigi Bosca is one of the most historically important wineries in Mendoza. Today the fourth generation of the Arizu family directs the largest growth in its history. In the international markets since 1984, Luigi Bosca helped pave the way for premium wines that have been developed in the last decade. In 1991, the original winery located in Lujan de Cuyo, an important sub-section of Mendoza, was updated and with the refinement of new premium brands, Luigi Bosca successfully became a very serious winemaker for many international markets. Today, the winery is very close to full capacity and its wines are of exceptional quality. Its introductory level of La Linda varietals are of very good quality for very accessible prices, under $10. Luigi Bosca makes 500,000 cases per year, with 50 % exported. Of the total cases, half are La Linda. In the local market, Luigi Bosca is a very important brand, as well.

The winery is tourist friendly and with reservations tours may be made. There is an excellent tasting area and store. www.luigibosca.com.ar

LUIGI BOSCA GALA 1 MALBEC 2006

COLOR   Purple
AROMA   Round fruity bouquet muted by oak, very inviting
BODY   Complex and delicious, very round, terrific berry mix
PALATE   Smooth and silky; milder fruits mute partially the strong Malbec
FINISH   Silky smooth, a delicious long lasting taste

GREAT

85% Malbec, 10% Petit Verdot, 5% Tannat 14 months in new French oak, 10,000 cases. A very serious wine, great value. Only wine I remember tasting with these 3 grapes which is based on the strength of Malbec but calmed by the other 2 reds. Wonderful. $35

LUIGI BOSCA GALA 2 CABERNET SAUVIGNON 2006

COLOR   Intense Purple
AROMA   Very inviting, berries and spices, oaken whiffs, Bordeaux like
BODY   Full, very masculine, complex mix of berries, minerals notes
PALATE   Very smooth, Delicious, French essence
FINISH   Velvet, delicious, long; voluptuous BLACK LACE

GREAT

80% Cabernet Sauvignon, 10% each Cab Franc/ Merlot. French in style, tropical in berries, this is a very serious and delicious wine Should be blind tasted against $150 California wines. $35

LUIGI BOSCA GALA 3 2007

COLOR   Yellow with green tinge
AROMA   Mild citrus, round and inviting
BODY   Medium Very interesting and rewarding,
           Refreshing
PALATE   Complex mix of grapes, delicious overtones of
           minerals and fruit
FINISH   Smooth, refreshing, delicious; Elegant

OUTSTANDING

50% Viognier, 40% Chardonnay, 10% Riesling; 5000 cases, $29

LUIGI BOSCA FINCA LOS NOBLES CHARDONNAY 2007

COLOR   Yellow with green tinges
AROMA   Round bouquet of citrus, mineral and fruits
           Very inviting
BODY   Medium, Very smooth and refreshing, Precise
           citrus tones
PALATE   Very round, firm taste of citrus, mineral laden;
           Opulent
FINISH   Even and smooth; juicy, refreshing and long
           lasting

OUTSTANDING

100% Chardonnay, from 90 year old vines in Las Compuertas; ideal for sole, swordfish, cod, halibut, $35

LUIGI BOSCA FINCA LOS NOBLES MALBEC-PETIT VERDOT 2005

COLOR   Intense Violet
AROMA   Inviting bouquet of muted berries
BODY   Full and round, Big, Well Structured,
PALATE   Very smooth, the petit verdot adds an elegant
           calming touch
FINISH   Silky smooth, delicious, long lasting

GREAT

Malbec and Petit Verdot planted together for over a century; approximately 86% malbec; 1550 cases; 20 months in French oak and another year in bottle. Single vineyard-Los Nobles, Terrific serious wine, $60

FINCA LOS NOBLES CABERNET SAUVIGNON BOUCHET 2005

COLOR   Very intense Purple
AROMA   Full and very inviting; an integrated
        smokiness
BODY   Full, very complex, Big wine, big fruits, Dense
PALATE   Big and strong; Sexy, delicious, Very round
        and structured
FINISH   Velvety smooth Masculine; powers through a
        long finish

GREAT
another serious wine, single vineyard-Los Nobles, very original in a series of 3 top wines; 82% Cab, 18% Bouchet (Similar to Cab Franc); 1300 6 pack cases; 24 months in French oak; around $60 VERY SPECIAL

LUIGI BOSCA MALBEC DOC 2006

COLOR   Rich full bouquet of berries; extremely
        inviting
AROMA   Enticing bouquet of dark berries
BODY   Full, smooth, silky, surprisingly elegant, well
        balanced
PALATE   Round, full Malbec blast; complex and
        enjoyable; great drinking wine
FINISH   Smooth Round velvety, Delicious

GREAT
100% Malbec, DOC means the precedence is audited by
the government as to location, percentage of grape and year; 70 year old vines 14 months in oak 3000 feet above sea level, single vineyard $26 Best value possible

LUIGI BOSCA EXTRA BRUT

COLOR   Yellow
AROMA   Champagne
BODY   Medium like French Champagne
PALATE   Delicious like the French
FINISH   Smooth and very enjoyable

OUTSTANDING
60% Chardonnay, 40% Pinot Noir, 10,000 cases, $30

LUIGI BOSCA ICONO 2006

COLOR Deep Purple
AROMA Very inviting, subtle
BODY   Full, round, masculine, Well-structured
PALATE Delicious, Dense with powerful red berries
       dominating
FINISH Velvet, sensuous, long lasting

GREAT

Malbec with Cab; single vineyard (Los Nobles in Las
Compuertas), 3300 feet above sea level, $80

MENDEL WINES

A true boutique winery, Mendel produces outstanding wines from the Lujan de Cuyo section of Mendoza. Mendel produces 6500 cases of Malbec based wines, with Roberto de la Mota, Argentina's most illustrious winemaker, responsible for this jewel and Santiago Mayorga Boaknin his talented assistant winemaker and vineyard manager. The winery is composed of two vineyards totaling 45 acres of 80 year old vines; one in Mayor Drummond (Lujan) and the other in Finca Remota (Uco Valley)--a little jewel! Owned by a family from Buenos Aires, led by Anabelle Sielecki, Mendel is named after the family's patriarch. www.mendel.com

MENDEL MALBEC 2007

COLOR	Intense Violet
AROMA	Big, full bouquet, lots of fruit, very inviting
BODY	Layers of fruit, superbly muted by oak; well-structured
PALATE	Full, Complex, Smooth, refreshing, delicious, Berries Galore
FINISH	Velvety smooth, Terrific

OUTSTANDING TO GREAT
only 5500 cases 12 months in French Oak, 100% Malbec. Preview of 2008, not yet bottled but should be as terrific as 2007. $30

MENDEL SEMILLON BLANC 2009

COLOR	Maize
AROMA	Citrus muted by oak Very inviting
BODY	Round, firm, delicious, mildly citric
PALATE	Smooth, muted grapefruit and laden with minerals
FINISH	Delicious and smooth

OUTSTANDING
Very original, 100% Semillon Blanc, $29

MENDEL UNUS 2006

COLOR   Intense Fuchsia

AROMA   Boldly complex and expressive, Very inviting

BODY   Full, extremely well balanced Complex and
        enjoyable

PALATE Lots of berries muted by oak, Ripe and
        powerful tannins

FINISH Very Sensual and smooth, Wonderful

GREAT

70% Malbec, 30% Cabernet Sauvignon 1000 cases; Aged 16 months in new
Taransaud French oak. Preview of 2008, young but should be great like 2007.
$60

MICHEL TORINO/EL ESTECO

Michel Torino is a century old company that is now a subsidiary of the Penaflor group. (See Trapiche for information on the largest wine company in the country) In Argentina, Michel Torino is synonymous for grocery store wine, so their premium wines are sold under the brand Esteco. However, in the U.S. Michel Torino is used.

The winery is located in the Northern mountains near the city of Salta, in the Cafayate Valley. Equipped with a state-of-the art infra-structure in a winery that was founded in 1898, the company produces 400,000 cases, with half exported and the rest consumed in Argentina. One line of the company is certified organic, the rest is not certified but uses sustainable procedures. I am told the only difference is the powder used to eradicate ants, which are a problem in the region. As the organic vineyards are small, organic solutions are used to rid them of ants.

The Winery is located at an altitude of over 5000 feet above sea level, with sun exposure of 350 days a year. The great thermal amplitude that results in warm days and cool nights creates grapes with even ripening and great concentration, With around 6 inches of rain a year, and rocky, sandy soil, the vines struggle to grow, thereby creating intense flavors. The water supply is through the runoff of the Andes melting of snow and is of the purest quality. The founders(1892), David Michel and his wife Gabriela Torino lend their name to the company and the Don David line is a homage to the patriarch. The winery has 700 hectares, with vines having an average age of 30 years. The starting levels of Coleccion and Cuma (organic) are good but the Don David Reserve and the Icon wine, Altimus are the ones we will look at closely.

The property has an exclusive Wine and Spa hotel, Patios de Cafayate, operated by Starwood/W, which opened in 2005, and a gourmet restaurant therein. The winery has a superb organic restaurant that prepares original dishes from the ages when the Incans ruled the area. Grilled llama, lamb, ancient dishes with quinoa, and many other delicacies are prepared in their original recipes with organically grown food. A 5 star spa completes a stay in this remote gem. Extremely tourist friendly with terrific infrastructure and interesting tours. www.esteco.com.ar; www.cumaorganic.com.ar; www.micheltorino.com.ar; www.Cocinadealtura.com.ar; info@cocinadealtura.com.ar

DON DAVID TORRONTES RESERVE 2008

COLOR   Pale Yellow
AROMA   Very inviting, smooth citrus/mineral/flower bouquet
BODY   Wonderfully smooth, muted flavors of citrus, flowers, minerals
PALATE   Complex and interesting; smooth; very refreshing, Dense
FINISH   Smooth as silk

GREAT

6 months for 10% in oak, 40 year old vines; 20,000 cases, Caution as great as this torrontes is, is it not clear how long it keeps its taste; buy all torrontes as young as possible. Here aging is a disadvantage! $16

DON DAVID MALBEC RESERVE 2007

COLOR   Violet
AROMA   Inviting, deep bouquet of flowers and berries
BODY   Very round, Full, almost chubby
PALATE   Extremely elegant, sensual, sophisticated, velvet smooth

OUTSTANDING TO GREAT

100% Malbec, 70% in oak for 1 year, 30,000 cases, $16

ALTIMUS 2005

COLOR   Almost Black
AROMA   Very Smooth, Bouquet of Berries, Flowers and Minerals
BODY   Very Full and Round; complex and elegant
PALATE   Excellent example of French style with Tropical Fruit
FINISH   Velvety smooth Fabulous

GREAT

A very serious wine; Altimus means highest(as in height and quality), only made when grapes are perfect; blend changes every year: 40% Cab, 35% Malbec, 15% Bonarda, 5% each Syran/Tannat; 1200 cases, 18 months in 1st use French Oak; An icon without a doubt, $35.

NAVARRO CORREAS

Navarro Correas is one of the oldest wineries in Argentina with a very rich history. Founded in 1798, the winery really began to take shape only in 1974 when Edmundo Navarro Correas, a descendant of the original founder, and a very successful politician, formally made it into a winery. Diageo, the spirits giant, with business world-wide bought it in 1996 and turned it into one of the most important wineries in the country. In 2009, the magnificent $20 million new winery was inaugurated in Perdriel, where the premium wines are being bottled. The original winery, 10 minutes from downtown Mendoza, in a quaint section called Godoy Cruz, has a 800 square foot visitor center, store and restaurant. The new facility is building its visitor center and should be of similar proportions. Navarro Correas won the Silver Medal for Wine Tourism by the Global Network Great Wine Controls. Both locations are fascinating, tourist-friendly and should not be missed. www.ncorreas.com

BODEGA SAN TELMO ESSENCIA TORRONTES 2009

COLOR   Pale Yellow with green nuances
AROMA   Very appealing citrus, principally grapefruit, inviting and round
BODY   Medium, surprisingly smooth, very refreshing
PALATE   Grapefruit and minerals; smooth but complex
FINISH   Delicious and smooth, Very refreshing. Great with sushi

OUTSTANDING
This is the entry level, but a very interesting wine. Terrific price, around $10, for a wonderful example of how to make Torrontes, second only to Malbec as an original Argentine wine.

NAVARRO CORREAS COLECCION PRIVADA---MALBEC 2008

COLOR   Deep Purple
AROMA   Mix of berries, flowers and minerals. Very intense and inviting
BODY   Medium to Full, Very smooth. Delicious
PALATE   Muted taste of berries; medium complexity; excellent malbec
FINISH   Smooth, easy to understand.

OUTSTANDING
100% Malbec 117,000 cases; easy to understand and delicious with tenderloin and other meats 30% 12 months in French oak, $15

ALLEGORIA CABERNET SAUVIGNON 2006

COLOR   Deep Purple
AROMA   Round, Full, Inviting
BODY   Big Fruit, Round and very smooth Delicious
PALATE   Gobs of Berries, Big and Bold, Complex and
          delicious
FINISH   Elegant and smooth; Easy

GREAT

A very complex wine that must breathe. Perhaps the best Allegoria yet made. 100% Cabernet 15 months in new French Oak

NAVARRO CORREAS ULTRA 2006

COLOR   Intense Violet, Almost Black
AROMA   Deep Berry Bouquet, Extremely inviting, very
          French
BODY   Full, complex, Elegant, Berries and Minerals, floral
          notes
PALATE   Velvety and delicious with muted Berry taste, with
          minerality, flowers
FINISH   Long lasting and elegant, smooth, sensual, subtle

GREAT

The best wine produced by Navarro Correas; 52% Malbec, 30% Cabernet Sauvignon, 18% Merlot. Around $39. A real pleasure of a French like, muted Malbec-Cab. Aged 100% in French oak for 18 months. Superb!!

NIETO SENETINER

The original winery was founded in 1888, making it one of the oldest in Mendoza. In 1969, the families Nieto and Senetiner purchased the vineyards and renamed it. In 1998, Perez Companc bought the winery and kept the name. Today it is incorporated into the Group Molinos Rio del Plata, Argentina's largest manufactured food company, producing soy products, processed oils, such as sunflower, margarine, etc. The winery has received the ISO quality standard for both 2001 and 2004 versions. Roberto Ganzalez is the talented head winemaker for over 18 years

Nieto Senetiner is extremely tourist friendly, having many special programs, as well as two beautiful wine tasting rooms, a boutique, and restaurant. Horse back riding up the mountains, where they serve hot chocolate and mate (a strong South American tea) with a magnificent view, is an exciting option; making your own wine labels, picking and cutting vines, are among many other wine related activities. Reservations essential.

Nieto Senetiner is very popular in Argentina, especially for its low priced wines. However, the winery is becoming very well known for its premium wines. Today, it exports 40% of its production, with a third of that to the U.S.
www.nietosentiner.com.ar

NIETO SENETINER DON NICANOR CHARDONNAY-VIOGNIER 2008

COLOR	Yellow with Green tinges
AROMA	Inviting citrus bouquet
BODY	Smooth citrus, notes of some sweet fruit; some complexity
PALATE	Mild lemony taste, very smooth, ideal for fish
FINISH	Very smooth and easy with mild citrus ending

OUTSTANDING
60% Chardonnay, 40% Viognier, 3 months in French oak, 11,000 cases of 6; $17.

DON NICANOR MALBEC 2007

COLOR	Almost Black
AROMA	Full Berry Bouquet with hints of spices and minerals
BODY	Round and Full; Dark Berries, a stand out
PALATE	Smooth and delicious
FINISH	Long and Smooth

VERY GOOD

100% Malbec, 1 year in oak, second use; 40,000 cases, with half consumed in country; 20% to U.S.; around $17

NIETO SENETINER BONARDA LIMITED EDITION 2007

COLOR   Fuschia
AROMA   Inviting bouquet of Berries and Minerals
BODY   Medium
PALATE   Smooth with lots of berries, some complexity
FINSIH   Mixed fruits; complex, interesting

VERY GOOD

2000 cases, aged 1 year in oak, 1 year in bottle; Argentina has 20,000 hectares of Bonarda, second largest quantity of plantations, losing only to Malbec. Traditionally, Bonarda has been used for mass-produced wine; today, many wineries are using Bonarda in premium wines, blended or individually, such as this limited edition. $25

NIETO SENETINER CADUS 2005

COLOR   Intense, deep Violet
AROMA   Extremely inviting Bouquet, strong on berries
         and minerals
BODY   BIG, Powerful, lots of complexity; Delicious
PALATE   Minerality gives a depth; complex, Fabulous
FINISH   Smooth, Complex, lovely end

GREAT

Far and away the company's best wine, their Icon; 100% Malbec, single vineyard, 40 year old vines; 2 years in French oak, from Agrelo; 3300 feet above sea level; Magnums available, $40

O. FOURNIER

Founded in 2000, O.Fournier is a modern, cutting-edge winery located in the La Consulta sector of Mendoza. Inspired by the stars and constellations in and around the Southern Cross, the wines made here are serious and complex.

Jose Manuel Ortega, the founder of the winery, is a former investment banker and very knowledgeable leader in the wine community. Equipped for fascinating wine tours, O.Fournier offers a fabulous gourmet restaurant with a terrific view of the Andes overlooking the expansive vineyard. Senora Ortega is the chef and does a fabulous job. The restaurant is open for lunch and a new version is opening downtown in Mendoza for dinner.

O. Fournier has vineyards in Spain and Chile, as well. Any serious wine aficionado should visit this winery and lunch in this modern structure with views galore. There are 7 rooms in the simple guest house he has on the property and can be previously reserved. O. Fournier is very tourist friendly.

The Urban Uco line is a wonderful inexpensive introduction to the varietals produced by the winery. www.ofournier.com; jmortega@ofournier.com

B CRUX SAUVIGNON BLANC 2008

COLOR	Pale maize
AROMA	Citrus and mineral tones implying complexity very inviting
BODY	Full and round; terrific mixture of citrus and minerality
PALATE	Complex, rewarding; light taste of lemon and pear; Smooth
FINISH	Smooth, with wonderful fruit. Delicious with sushi

OUTSTANDING

only 500 cases; Uco valley. Fermented and aged in Stainless Steel tanks; 100% varietal. $18

B CRUX RED 2005

COLOR	Very Dark Purple
AROMA	Very inviting Full, Round Berry Bouquet
BODY	Medium to Full, Smooth; mix of berry and minerals
PALATE	Very smooth, muted Berry taste
FINISH	Smooth, Delicious

OUTSTANDING

60% Tempranillo, 35% Malbec, 5% Syrah 3500 cases. 1 year in oak. $24

ALFA CRUX 2004

COLOR   Deep Violet
AROMA   Smokey fruits; Extremely inviting, sensuous
BODY   Complex and Full; Lots of Fruit muted by oak;
          Excellent
PALATE   Interesting and complex; Smooth; Velvety,
          Fruit and minerals
FINISH   Smooth, lasting, wonderfully elegant

GREAT

50% Tempranillo, 30% Malbec, 20% Merlot. 2700 cases; 17 months in new oak barrels. Around $42.

ALFA CRUX MALBEC 2006

COLOR   Black
AROMA   Fragrant; smoky fruit bouquet; very inviting
BODY   Silky and smooth, Full and round. Sumptuous
          Character
PALATE   Lots of Berries-Minerals, Malbec and oak,
          Unusually Elegant
FINISH   Velvet Smooth, Lasting

GREAT

100% Malbec, Around $45 1000 cases; 20 months in oak; Unfiltered, Wonderful example of how Malbec should taste, $60

O FOURNIER SYRAH MALBEC 2005

COLOR   Intense Purple, almost Black
AROMA   Smoky wood and berries, with mineral
          overtones, Inviting
BODY   Very Full and Round, with the feel of wood and
          berries
PALATE   Strong and Complex, Masculine, Smoothed
          by Syrah and oak
FINISH   Silky and smooth; very interesting and
          delicious

GREAT

50% Syrah, Malbec; only 270 cases double selection by hand, Fermentation in Stainless Steel tanks, Aging 20 months in oak No filtration very special, $80

O. FOURNIER 2008

COLOR   Black
AROMA   Subtle and inviting
BODY   Complex, great Syrah
PALATE   Complex mix of spices and berries, Floral
         notes. Very smooth
FINISH   Velvety, delicious

GREAT

100% Syrah, only 230 cases. Around $80

PASCUAL TOSO

Founded in 1890, by Pascual Toso, an Italian winemaker from Piamonte, this winery has a rich tradition. With two vineyards, one in Maipu, the other in San Jose, Pascual Toso is known today as a producer of excellent wines, with over 400,000 cases per annum. Paul Hobbs has been a consultant since 2001 and Rolando Luppino is the head winemaker. Las Barrancas, the 400 hectare vineyard in Maipu, produces their premium wines. Las Barrancas has an elevation of over 2000 feet. The San Jose winery, just minutes from downtown Mendoza, produces 700,000 cases of sparkling wines.

They accept visitors with previous reservations.
tosowines@bodegastoso.com.ar; info@bodegastoso.com.ar

PASCUAL TOSO TORRONTES 2008

COLOR   Light Yellow
AROMA   Muted Citrus
BODY   Full, Flowers complement Citrus fruits,
        whiffs of jasmine
PALATE Surprisingly smooth and round, dense, Very
        Interesting
FINISH Smooth, long, very refreshing

VERY GOOD TO OUTSTANDING
100% Torrontes, from Las Barrancas, still rare to find Torrontes produced with grapes from Mendoza, $12

PASCUAL TOSO MALBEC ROSE 2009

COLOR   Bright Rose
AROMA   Subtle bouquet of spicy fruit
BODY   Medium, some mild sweetness, Round
PALATE Very refreshing, interesting and delicious
FINISH Long, smooth, Very enjoyable

OUTSTANDING
100% Malbec, one of the best roses from South America, $12

PASCUAL TOSO MALBEC 2008

COLOR   Dark Purple
AROMA Inviting berry bouquet with touches of spices
BODY   Big. Full, Round, very enjoyable
PALATE Tasty fruits with layers of variety, complex, dense
FINISH   Smooth, long, languid

OUTSTANDING
100% Malbec, 40% in American oak for 6 months, $12

PASCAL TOSO MALBEC RESERVE 2007

COLOR   Dark Purple
AROMA Inviting subtle tones of red berries
BODY   Very full, Layers of berries, Dense
PALATE Lots of fruits, smoky, Round, well structured
FINISH   Long, very smooth, Delicious

OUTSTANDING
100% Malbec, 1 year in oak, 80% French,20% American, $20

PASCUAL TOSO FINCA PEDREGAL 2005

COLOR   Deep Purple
AROMA Subtle hints of berries and flowers
BODY   Full, Structured, Dense
PALATE Round, layers of fruit, complex,
FINISH   Delicious, long and smooth

OUTSTANDING
70% Malbec, 30% Cab, 100% in oak for 18 months, Cab in American and Malbec in French, $60.

POESIA

A wonderful gem of a winery owned by Helene Garcin, a successful winery owner in France and run by Chagneau Herve, a dynamic and talented wine-maker, Poesia produces very high quality wines with a French touch and tropical grapes from old vines. Among Madame Garcin's holdings in France is Clos l'Eglise in Pommerol and Chateau Bard Haut in St. Emilion. Poesia will soon be known to be in this elite category. All of the wines urgently need to have 40 minutes open prior to drinking in order to reach ultimate tasting pleasure. First vintage was 2001.

POESIA PASODOBLE 2007

COLOR   Crimson
AROMA   Round, inviting, supple fruit and floral notes
BODY   Medium accessible, Delightful
PALATE   Berries and minerals with floral overtones
FINISH   Smooth as silk Subtle and rewarding

OUTSTANDING
8000 cases, 55% Malbec, 35% Syrah, 10% Bonarda $10

CLOS DES ANDES RESERVA 2006

COLOR   Intense fuschia
AROMA   Supple Fruit, Very Round, Inviting
BODY   Medium and Young, Needs Aging but is still terrific
PALATE   Smooth, Fruity with lots of minerals, Well-Structured
FINISH   Smooth, lots of fruit

OUTSTANDING
100% Malbec, aged in oak 16 months, Will be even better with aging very interesting wine, $24

POESIA 2005

COLOR	Black
AROMA	Very Full, inviting notes of fruit and minerals Complex
BODY	Full, Muted Berries, Minerals floral touches from Malbec
PALATE	Very Round, Gobs of fruits, tannins, Big wine, terrific density
FINISH	Smooth, French, Long-Lasting

GREAT

requires lots of aeration; 60% Malbec, 40% Cabernet Sauvignon, about 1200 cases 12-18 months in oak. All years from 2003 to 2008 were tasted, the latter out of the barrel as it is not yet bottled. Clearly this wine improves with age, although the later years are the best, as the winemakers acquired knowledge about their grapes, planting, time of harvest and many other details. I believe Poesia's icon will improve with aging in the bottle and ultimately, the 2008 will be the best of the group. A magnificent effort! $48

POESIA UNAMED ICON (not yet bottled or named—will be released in 2011) 2008

COLOR	Deep violet, almost black
AROMA	Brimming with fruit and floral notes
BODY	Full and very round Structured
PALATE	After only 3 months in barrels, great fruit and smooth tones
FINISH	Incredibly smooth and delicious

GREAT

this will be a superb wine 100% Malbec single vineyard Uco Valley, Will have some 600 cases. Will be a collector's item and a true pleasure

SALENTEIN

One of the more interesting and controversial projects in Mendoza, Salentein winery is located in the most desert like section of Uco Valley, 62 miles south of Mendoza city. With 4900 acres at the dramatic base of the Andes, the winery has developed vines on 1124 acres. At the entrance way is the chapel of Gratitud, further on is a 900 acre nature preserve; additionally there is a guest house open to the public, 2 restaurants and a wine shop.

Absolutely captivating is the art museum and art gallery, both of which exhibit modern and ancient art, much of which is Argentine. All of the above is built with local materials, principally stone and give one the feeling of scenes out of the Da Vinci Code. Tourists are welcomed warmly and the multi-lingual staff is anxious to show one around and explain all the attractions. Art lovers and nature lovers should leave a lot of time to explore and even stay over night at the 16 room posada.

The Posada gourmet restaurant overlooks the pinot noir and merlot vineyards, with dramatic views of the Andes. The winery itself is in the shape of a cross and has three large tasting rooms with travertine tables from a nearby quarry. The architecture has won various international awards. I could have spent a lot more time wandering the rooms underground.

Salentein offers various entry level lines of wine that range from good to very good. Below are the stars of the winery's lineup.
www.bodegasalentein.com; posada@bodegasalentein.com

SALENTEIN PRIMUM PINOT NOIR 2004

COLOR | Purple
AROMA | Smoky oak infused berry bouquet; light and enticing
BODY | Medium, fruity, very smooth and elegant; not complex
PALATE | Smooth, easy to understand, no complexity, straightforward
FINISH | Velvety smooth; Very feminine

OUTSTANDING
100% Pinot Noir; 4500 feet above sea level; aged in oak for 1 year. Called Primus in Argentina and many European countries, Primum in U.S. A drink for couples

SALENTEIN PRIMUM MALBEC 2005

COLOR | Black
AROMA | Full, muted Berry bouquet in oak
BODY | Full, strong fruit, lots of oak,
PALATE | Delicious, with lots of fruit, very straightforward

FINISH   Smooth Easy, big fruit

OUTSTANDING

100% Malbec 19 months in oak, 1 year in bottle; 1500 cases; potentially great with some more aging;

SALENTEIN NUMINA 2005

COLOR   Deep Violet
AROMA   Smoky fruit, Interesting
BODY   Full, very interesting, complex, smoothed by
         the merlot and the oak
PALATE   Delicious, complex, Full Body, but not
         overpowering Smooth
FINISH   Smooth, clean, long finish

GREAT

60% Malbec, 40% Merlot; 16 months in oak, Uco valley; the best of the winery; however, there have been subsequent vintages of Numina that did not maintain this quality. 2004 is the year so far. The Icon of the winery.

TERRAZAS DE LOS ANDES

Established in 1999, Terrazas is a premier wine maker and subsidiary of Moet Hennessy of France. Originally built in 1898 by Sotero Arizu, one of the founders of wine making in Argentina, Terrazas carefully restored the Spanish style winery and its magnificent vineyards.

Today, facing the Cordon del Plata section of the Andes mountains, and located in the Perdriel division of Mendoza, Terrazas produces outstanding wines from century old vineyards. With average altitude of 3500 feet and as the largest landowner in Vistalba, Terrazas not only makes great Malbecs but has a series of white wines as well.

Terrazas is Spanish for terraces, which is how most of the Malbec is planted on the mountainside. There is a lovely 6 room residence in the main house. Tours and lunch can be had with previous reservations. www.terrazasdelosandes.com

TERRAZAS TORRONTES RESERVA 2008

COLOR   Pale Maize
AROMA   Inviting, wonderful bouquet of citrus
         (grapefruit) and minerals
BODY   Complex and delicious; surprisingly smooth
         and round.
PALATE   Very refreshing, smooth; muted tasted of
         grapefruit and minerals
FINISH   Elegant, smooth, sensuous. Superior to
         Riesling, best with food;

OUTSTANDING
First vintage; to be sold in 2010 in U. S., From Cafayate Valley, Salta, 5600 feet above sea level, branch covered pergola protects against strong mountain sun, $16, as are all the reservas

TERRAZAS RESERVA MALBEC 2006

COLOR   Intense Violet
AROMA   Full Bouquet of cherries and flowers; very
         inviting
BODY   Big berry taste muted by oak, very well
         structured
PALATE   Complex and smooth, layers of dark berries;
         Dense, Delicious
FINISH   Powerful and round, Very long, wonderful

OUTSTANDING
100% Malbec, 50% from Uco Valley, 50% from Vistalba, I year in oak, $18

TERRAZAS AFINCADO MALBEC 2005

COLOR   Intense Violet
AROMA   Very inviting Berry Bouquet freshened by flowers
BODY   Full, Complex Big but elegant
PALATE   Smooth, very round, Elegantly Complex
FINISH   Smooth as silk; wonderful taste that keeps on
           coming SENSUAL!

GREAT
100% Malbec from Vistalba, made of the best grapes of the
vineyard not used by Cheval Interesting side story: When
French winemakers first started planting, they wanted all Malbec removed,
to be replaced by Pinot Noir. The workers, many of whom still are active,
did not obey and kept the best Malbec planted. When the French tasted the
final product, they agreed to leave Malbec in the wine, including Cheval des
Andes. Today, the product is the best of the French knowledge and history,
with the best grapes Mendoza produces—a true blend of cultures. $45

TERRAZAS AFINCADO CABERNET SAUVIGNON 2005

COLOR   Intense Purple
AROMA   Extremely inviting bouquet of Berries
BODY   Big, round, elegant, Muted berry, flowers and
           minerals
PALATE   Subtle mixture of Berries, Flowers, minerals.
           Very elegant, smooth
FINISH   Wonderful, velvety smooth; Elegant

GREAT
Price: $45

TERRAZAS AFINCADO TARDIO 2004

COLOR   Deep Maize
AROMA   Soft Orange—Inviting flowery bouquet
BODY   Delicate, mildly sweet
PALATE   Subtle, lightly sweet desert wine complex combo of
           flowers, orange
FINISH   Elegant, silky smooth, lightly sweet

GREAT
Petit Monsant, after dinner wine, $25

TRAPICHE

Trapiche is the largest exporter of wines from Argentina, producing over 2.5 million cases a year, of which 1.4 million are exported to over 80 countries. Trapiche is, in turn, owned by the PenaFlor group, which is the country's largest producer of wines. Formerly owned by the Pulenta family, the group is owned today by DLJ South American Partners.

In November, 2008 Trapiche inaugurated its newly reformed, hi tech winery, which was celebrating 125 years since its founding. A tour of the winery is fascinating, as Trapiche has preserved much of the original structure and many of the old wine-making tools. It is a magnificent mixture of cutting-edge modern technology within the centennial walls and the accoutrements of a beautiful landmark building.

Daniel Pi, chief winemaker, has brilliantly led the creation of new premium wine concepts and a spectacular growth in the last 6 years. Today, its top wines can compete in any market.

Trapiche is quite tourist friendly and a trip to the newly inaugurated winery is time well spent. Guided tours are in Spanish or English, and are complemented by tastings, a boutique and wine sales. visitas@trapiche.com.ar

TRAPICHE MALBEC 2003

COLOR	Intense violet
AROMA	Medium to full, lots of berries and minerals
BODY	Medium for Malbec but smooth and easy Round tasting
PALATE	Round and tasty medium complexity, easy to grasp
FINISH	Smooth Berries and minerals, notes of flowers

VERY GOOD
at around $8, fantastic buy. Leading product in Trapiche's introductory line; 12 varietals in their low priced range.

TRAPICHE OAK CASK PINOT NOIR 2008

COLOR	Violet
AROMA	Smooth, Flowery, berries and minerals
BODY	Smooth, medium complexity, easy to understand, with a slight sweetness
PALATE	Smooth, straight forward
FINISH	Smooth with an easy languishing style

VERY GOOD
The oak cask series is the next step up , 6 varietals aged for 12 months in oak. Malbec, Cabernet Sauvignon Syrah, Merlot, and Chardonnay are the others in the group. At around $11, another great buy. 50,000 cases of each.

TRAPICHE BROQUEL BONARDA 2007

COLOR   Dark violet
AROMA   Round and inviting
BODY   Medium to full; lots of fruit
PALATE Smooth, opens slowly, not complex
FINISH Smooth and easy to drink Italian meat sauce
        on Pasta is ideal

OUTSTANDING
Terrific winemaking, preserving the terroir and originality of the Bonarda grape. Originally from Savoie, France, Bonarda has flourished in Argentina and will be a major force in future harvests. Still new to U.S. it should be tried in the best Italian restaurants. The Broquel line of 8 are around $14 and are mind boggling great buys. (see below)

TRAPICHE BROQUEL TORRONTES 2008

COLOR   Very Pale Yellow
AROMA   Smooth very round citrus, Extremely inviting
BODY   Somewhat complex, lots of citrus and
        minerals refreshing
PALATE Complex minerality, layers of fruit creating a
        very interesting wine
FINISH Fruity, interesting and fun

OUTSTANDING
Again capturing terroir represented by a terrific torrontes, great with fish dishes and spices., $15

TRAPICHE BROQUEL MALBEC 2007

COLOR   Intense Violet
AROMA   Mixed berries, notes of flowers and minerals
BODY   Full, smooth very enjoyable; complex; lots of
        berries, minerals
PALATE Good Complexity, fruity, muted by oak;
        Notes of flowers, spices
FINISH Smooth and delicious Must breathe 30 minutes

OUTSTANDING
100% Malbec from Uco Valley, Agrelo sector, 2001 had 4000 cases, now 50,000; (over 12 times increase); 15 months in oak from 20 year old vines. Crazy inexpensive at $15. Broquel produces Cabernet Franc, Cabernet Sauvignon, Petit Verdot, and Chardonnay, besides the ones evaluated herein.

TRAPICHE BROQUEL PINOT NOIR 2007

COLOR   Fuschia
AROMA   Medium flowers and berries; extremely inviting
BODY   Medium to full; smooth and delicious
PALATE   Smooth, extremely round terrific Pinot
FINISH   Languishing delight, smooth and long-lasting Couple's dream

GREAT

The best Broquel, just superb! At $15, everyone should have a case. Only 2,000 cases. This will be a big seller if properly marketed in the states

TRAPICHE LAS PALMAS CHARDONNAY 2007

COLOR   Yellow with green tinges
AROMA   Wonderful, inviting, burgundian bouquet, flowers and minerals
BODY   Round, full, subtle, with tropical muted citrus
PALATE   Delicious, complex, subtle with minerals and classic French touch
FINISH   Silky smooth and sensuous

GREAT

This is superb, very French, all time great Chardonnay. Will last and age well for a decade, as promised by the winemaker's orientation. $22

TRAPICHE FINCA LAS PALMAS CABERNET SAUVIGNON 2007

COLOR   Intense violet
AROMA   Round, full bodied, inviting
BODY   Smooth, medium complexity with lots of fruit muted by oak,
PALATE   Full Easy, muted berries and minerals
FINISH   Smooth and Velvety

OUTSTANDING

100% Cabernet Sauvignon. Very smooth and subtle $27

TRAPICHE MALBEC SINGLE VINEYARDS 2006

Vina Cristina y Bibiana Coletto
Vina Federico Villafane
Vina Adriana Venturin

COLOR   Deep Purple

AROMA   All are very round and inviting the 3rd being more complex

BODY   All are full and complex, lots of berries muted by oak; the 3rd is fullest

PALATE   All smooth, Round, Sensual, 2nd somewhat more interesting

FINISH   Smooth Velvety, 3rd more sensuous and silky

GREAT

Winemaker Daniel Pi depends on many vineyards for his Malbecs and he decided to honor each year the 3 best Malbecs his suppliers offer by labeling their wine as single vineyards for Trapiche. All 3 are fabulous in 2006, with Adriana Venturin's effort a little ahead of the others. They are all around $49 and are wonderful

TRAPICHE ISCAY 2006

COLOR   Intense Violet

AROMA   Big, round, very French

BODY   Complex, smooth, Big and delicious

PALATE   Tremendous taste of berries and minerals floral notes; Round

FINISH   Smooth, Sophisticated Bordeaux characteristics

GREAT

Originally aided by Michelle Roland, Iscay is now under the complete direction of Daniel Pi. Iscay (means two in Quechuan, the original language of the Incas) The wine is named in honor of the Argentine land combined with the European heritage that handed down through generations the art of wine creation; also, two grapes make up the blend. 50-50 Merlot-Malbec, aged 18 months in new French oak; $70

TRAPICHE MANOS MALBEC 2004

COLOR Black
AROMA Muted Berries
BODY Very full and complex; lots of grapes,
 developed by French oak
PALATE Smooth, subtle, complex
FINISH Delicious Easy languid smooth

GREAT

Manos means hands and is a tribute to the workers who make a double selection of the grapes; 100% Malbec and one of the best. 24 months in new French oak and 24 months in bottles. The Icon of the winery, all grapes are from Uco Valley; This is the first vintage and it is a masterpiece. $100

TRIVENTO

Trivento is the second largest exporting winery in Argentina, behind Penaflor, with 2,500,000 cases of wine produced annually and about 70% exported. Owned by Chilean giant, Concha y Toro, Trivento is trying to raise its quality as its parent has done so well. Trivento "means three winds" and refers to the currents passing through the Lujan de Cuyo sub-section of Mendoza area.

Trivento has many outstanding wines, after many years as a bulk wine producer. Federico Galdeano is the winemaker since 1997, when Trivento initiated its wine production. Ultra premium wines began in 2002.

In 2007, Trivento invested $15 million, most of which was dedicated to building a winery solely for premium wines and upgrading the state of the art vineyard equipment. On my visit, in 2009, the winery was still not totally finished. Trivento has 3,185 hectares of vineyards in the Mendoza area. Its Premium wines continue to improve and develop. Available in 100 countries around the world. www.trivento.com; sbarros@trivento.com

TRIVENTO AMADO SUR 2007

COLOR   Purple
AROMA   Some complexity, Inviting bouquet of various
        berries
BODY   Medium to Full, mix of fruits, spices and minerals
PALATE Smooth, easy, fruity
FINISH Smooth, Easy

VERY GOOD
72% Malbec, 16% Bonarda, 12% Syrah; Amado Sur means "beloved South". 8 months in French oak, then 6 months in stainless steel, $15

TRIVENTO GOLDEN RESERVE CHARDONNAY 2008

COLOR   Pale Yellow
AROMA   Inviting citrus bouquet
BODY   Smooth, refreshing
PALATE Fruits and minerals combine here in a
        smooth, chewy taste
FINISH Smooth, easy, citrus dominant ending

VERY GOOD
3RD Vintage; 12 months in French oak, 1000 cases, Tropical fruits are the primary taste, $15

TRIVENTO GOLDEN RESERVE SYRAH 2006

COLOR   Purple
AROMA   Inviting, medium bouquet of berries and
            spices
BODY   Pleasing, Medium Body
PALATE   Smooth and even, will get even better with a
            few years aging
FINISH   Smooth, berry ending

VERY GOOD
made from 80 year old vines; 100% Syrah, $22

TRIVENTO GOLDEN RESERVE MALBEC 2006

COLOR   Dark Purple
AROMA   Full Body bouquet of Berries, Spices and
            minerals
BODY   Very smooth, lots of berries and spices, muted
            by oak
PALATE   Full, delicious; berries/spices combo, medium
            complexity
FINISH   Smooth ending with muted berries/minerals/spices

OUTSTANDING
Best of Golden Reserve group; 100% Malbec, 90% in French Oak, 10% in
American oak; good buy at $22

TRIVENTO EOLO 2006

COLOR   Dark Fuchsia
AROMA   Full bouquet of berries/minerals
BODY   Elegant, Full, Lots of Fruit, muted by oak
PALATE   Smooth, delicious,
FINISH   Elegant and smooth

OUTSTANDING
90% Malbec, 10% Syrah, Vines planted in 1912, means
"keeper of the winds", 80% in new French oak; around $75

TRIVENTO BRISA DE OTONO 2008

COLOR   Maize
AROMA   Bouquet of sweet fruits
BODY   Delicious and sweet
PALATE   Easy to comprehend; lots of fruits, delicious
FINISH   Smooth, sweet, great way to end a meal

OUTSTANDING
800 Cases, name means "Autumn Breeze", great with cheese
and fruits at end of meal; $17

VINA COBOS

One of the more interesting projects in Mendoza, Vina Cobos is the combined invention of the now legendary Paul Hobbs, known primarily in wine circles for his California wines, but also a very serious consultant who has influenced numerous wineries around South America, and the heirs of the Marchiori vineyards in Mendoza. The latter vineyards, which have been in the Marchiori family for four decades, are located in the sub-section of Mendoza called Perdriel, a great micro-climate at the foothills of the Andes.

Paul Hobbs has been connected to Mendoza since 1989 and has consulted on major vineyards like Catena Zapata where he was a key consultant for the great Chardonnays they have produced and Pascual Toso, where the Malbecs are curiously similar to those of Vina Cobos. These wines are characterized by a very smooth, round taste, which is rich in flavor.

The winery is tourist friendly and tours can be had by appointment. info@paulhobbs.com

VINA COBOS FELINO CABARNET SAUVIGNON 2007

COLOR   Intense violet
AROMA   Full, round, inviting bouquet of muted dark
         berries/minerals
BODY   Full, Very smooth, complex and interesting
PALATE   Round, dense, and delicious, smooth taste of
         muted berries
FINISH   Very long close; special

OUTSTANDING
86% Cab, 14% divided among merlot, malbec, syrah, and petit verdot; aged 9 months in French and American oak of which 22% is new; Felino means cat, $25

VINA COBOS FELINO MALBEC 2008

COLOR   Intense Violet
AROMA   Inviting bouquet of Berry, Spice, Minerals; Full
BODY   Full, Very Smooth, Very Round Delicious
PALATE   Round, Very Big; Lots of fruit but a real wine!
FINISH   Smooth, Long and languid. Superb

OUTSTANDING TO GREAT
91% Malbec, 6% Cab, 3% Syrah; 8 months in oak, 21% new; Malbec from both Uco Valley and Lujan de Cuyo, Unusually great value, $25

BRAMARE CHARDONNAY MARCHIORI 2007

COLOR   Maize
AROMA   Full, inviting aroma of pears/sweet citrus
BODY   Very smooth, slight sweetness, Full and complex
PALATE   Big and full; round marginally sweet citrus/ fruits; delicious
FINISH   Smooth, very long, superb

GREAT
10 months in French oak, 58% new; 10 year old vines; 100% Chardonnay, Bramare means to yearn for, symbolic of the winery's desire to produce extraordinary wine; $35

BRAMARE CABERNET SAUVIGNON MARCHIORI 2006

COLOR   Deep purple
AROMA   Inviting and full
BODY   Big, Fruity, Very Full, great structure
PALATE   Very smooth, Like Silk, berries, minerals, spices
FINISH   Long, smooth, Sensual

OUTSTANDING TO GREAT
18 Months in American oak, 37% new; 100% Cab, $$80

BRAMARE MALBEC MARCHIORI 2006

COLOR   Purple, almost black
AROMA   Inviting Bouquet of Dark Berries, Spices, Minerals
BODY   Complex, Full, Lots of Fruit
PALATE   Round, Big Berry Taste, Structured
FINISH   Smooth extremely long, Delicious

GREAT

100% Malbec, 18 months in French and American oak, 65% new, 50 year old vines; single vineyard; unfined and unfiltered (as all of their red wines), $80

COBOS MALBEC 2006

COLOR   Black
AROMA   Round, extremely inviting
BODY   Very Full, Very Round, Extraordinary
PALATE   Velvety Smooth, Muted Berries, Spices, Bordeaux like
FINISH   Smooth, long lasting, Silky, Sensual

GREAT

100% Malbec, 80 year old vines, Single vineyard, Super selective, hand picked, 18 months in 88% new French oak, conceived to be the essence of Mendoza terroir and pure Malbec character; it achieves that, $160

COBOS NICO 2006

COLOR   Intense Violet, almost black
AROMA   Enticing whiffs of dark berries
BODY   Velvet glove of large berries, Structured, Layers of Fruit
PALATE   Extraordinarily smooth, Muted Berries predominate
FINISH   Very long, delicious, Sensual

GREAT

63% Cab, 37% Malbec, Single vineyard, oak aged, $175

VISTALBA: FINCA E POSADA
CARLOS PULENTA

One of the newest and most modern wineries in Mendoza, set in 57 year old vineyards, Vistalba is the creation of Carlos Pulenta, a member of the Pulenta family that owned PenaFlor, Argentina's largest wine company. With 53 hectares, the planting of which terminated in 1999, Vistalba has plantations of Malbec, Merlot, Cabernet Sauvignon and Bonarda. With an average elevation of just under 3000 feet, the magnificent estate contains a breath-taking new winery, a beautiful Inn (Posada) and a very chic, French style restaurant, Le Bourgogne.

Tourist friendly, Vistalba is a must see winery, with wonderful wines. Carlos Pulenta is the knowledgeable and charming owner; a great story teller and host, who knows the history of each important vineyard in the Mendoza area, many of which he consulted for prior to building his own. Reservations essential. Take home their olive oil, rich and pure. The winery offers 2 lines of wine, the Tomeros, and the Vistalba Corte A, B, and C. www.carlospulentawines.com

TOMERO CHARDONNAY 2008

COLOR   Yellow with tinges of green
AROMA   Citrus muted by oak
BODY   Smooth, light, refreshing, Bouquet of Citrus;
         laden with minerals
PALATE   Lemony light, very refreshing; steely crisp,
         touch of vanilla
FINISH   Smooth citrus, long lasting Ideal for fish

OUTSTANDING
8 months in oak, 2000 cases, 30 year old vines, around $12

TOMERO TORRONTES 2009

COLOR   Pale Yellow
AROMA   Lots of flowers, citrus, a little honey, very
         enticing
BODY   Full, complex, exciting floral notes, great
         structure
PALATE   Big with lots of personality; very enjoyable and round
FINISH   Flowers like a field with citrus sprinkled around, smooth

OUTSTANDING
100% Torrontes, match to fish and sushi, $12

TOMERO SAUVIGNON BLANC 2008

COLOR Pale Maize
AROMA Inviting bouquet of citrus and minerals
BODY Very smooth, embedded citrus, Elegant, Burgundian
PALATE Smooth, Full, Round, Minerals and fruits, Delicious
FINISH Velvety Smooth, serious, delicious wine

GREAT
100% Sauvignon Blanc, not yet sold in U.S., vines planted in 1996. A real treat!

TOMERO PETIT VERDOT RESERVA 2006

COLOR Purple
AROMA Very inviting; Berries surround some mineral tones
BODY Big, Round, Elegant
PALATE Very smooth, Terrific minerality; elegant layers of berry;
FINISH Sensuous, smooth, Terrific long lasting

OUTSTANDING
100% Petit Verdot,15 months in French oak, $26

TOMERO MALBEC GRAN RESERVA 2006

COLOR Intense Violet
AROMA Intoxicating Bouquet of Berries Very appealing
BODY Wonderfully Full Bodied and Smooth, Complex, Dense
PALATE Big, Round, multiple berry and spice layers, Bold, Delicious
FINISH Smooth, Very Elegant, Top Notch

GREAT
3rd vintage, 20 months in French oak, very structured $48

VISTALBA CORTE B 2005

COLOR   Purple
AROMA   Inviting, lots of berries
BODY   Medium to Full, Berries, Minerals, Spices, Great
        mix, well- structured
PALATE Round, Berries muted by oak Very elegant, some
        complexity
FINISH Smooth and silky

OUTSTANDING
60% Malbec, 30% Bonarda, 10% Cab; 1 year in French oak,
20 months in bottles, $28

VISTALBA CORTE A 2006

COLOR   Intense Violet
AROMA   Big and round, fruity, very inviting
BODY   Very Full, very smooth, Dense and Balanced,
        Wonderful
PALATE Smooth, complex, Opulent use of berries and
        minerals, Elegant
FINISH Velvety smooth,

GREAT
85% Malbec, 15% Cab, Very serious wine, delicious, 18
months in new French oak, $45

PROGENIE BRUT

COLOR   Champagne/amber
AROMA   Light and fruity
BODY   Tastes like a top-notch French
        Champagne
PALATE Smooth, bubbly, mild citrus
FINISH Delicious, perfect amount of bubbles

OUTSTANDING
very French in style and taste, $50

Chile

Chile

Chile is a long, narrow coastal strip that is bordered by the majestic Andes mountains on the East and the extremely cold Pacific Ocean on the West. Chile has an average width of only 174 kilometers(109 miles), but is 2700 miles long. Chile's largest export is copper, which is mostly found in the desert area of the north, and which has brought large foreign companies to the country. The Northern half of the country is desert with some oases of agriculture. The central area is the political and economic hub, with many of the important vineyards being within an hour from Santiago, its capital city.

The Spanish Conquistadores (Conquerors) came to Chile in the mid-16th century on their endless search for gold. Prior to the Spanish arrival, the land was ruled by the Incans, with the indigenous Araucanians inhabiting the central and Southern areas. Winemaking began in the 1550's to produce wine for the church celebration of the sacraments. The Pais grape (Pah ees), similar to the mission grapes of California, was planted by the Spanish missionaries. These roots survived centuries without irrigation or viticulture. Truly, they were the first organic grapes of the new world.

Gradually, these vines were brought to other sections of the country and a budding industry began to take hold. Large landholders brought vines from Spain at first, then more importantly, France. In the 1830's, the first vitis vinifera was planted in Chile. Sixty varieties were brought to Chile by the new Quinta Normal campus of the University of Chile.

By the 1850's, many of the important grapes of Bordeaux had been planted in Chile, principally in the Central Valley. Cabernet Sauvignon and Sauvignon Blanc predominated. A booming economy allowed some of the more successful industrialists and large landholders to begin to commercialize their wine. The beginnings of many of today's wineries took hold at that time. When the Phylloxera plague devastated Europe, in the mid 1860's, most especially Bordeaux, many workers came to Chile and the industry grew immensely. Due in part to Chile's climate, in part to a vigilant government in ensuring that sick plants are not imported to Chile, and in part to luck, Chile has never had significant disease affecting agriculture. As a result, the need for chemical usage is minimal and sustainable policies are the norm. Organic and bio-dynamic wineries are becoming the goal to achieve.

Before the Panama Canal, Chile was isolated from the rest of the world, as would-be travelers had to go around Brazil and Argentina, past Tierra del Fuego, prior to turning North to get to Chile. Economically, it was easier to trade with the other countries than making the long trip around. An interesting footnote is Chile's claim to over 480,000 square miles of Antarctica. Also, other than Ecuador, Chile is the only country in South America that does not border Brazil. The opening of the Panama Canal was crucial to Chile's economic growth, especially to its budding viniculture business

Chile achieved independence in 1810, but only rid themselves of the Spanish 8 years later. Subsequently, in the War of the Pacific, they annexed lands that were part of Peru and Bolivia to the North. By the 1880's, the Indians were totally subjugated and placed on uncivilized reservations in the far South, where they still live today. Various political policies over the next hundred years kept the country's wine industry from developing. A land reform act inhibited growth into new areas.

Chile has traditionally been coup-free, with the exception of the Nixon-backed military takeover in 1973. The repressive Pinochet-led military government ruled until a democratically elected government took power in 1990.

As bad as Pinochet may have been socially and politically, Chile became a First-World country economically and, with a very stable economy and changes of laws with regard to agriculture, the wine industry among others, began to flourish. After Pinochet's changes, agriculture and wine industries blossomed. As if wakened from a century long sleep, Chile's wine industry expanded dramatically in various parts of the country. Seemingly overnight, there was a radical growth in the number of plantations for food and wine. Soon premium wines became the goal and, with many foreign investors starting or buying vineyards, Chile's exports grew significantly. Until this time, bulk wines were the norm and most were consumed internally. Giant groups like Concha y Toro, San Pedro, and Santa Rita turned from producing only bulk wines to creating sophisticated state of the art wineries, thereby producing upscale, premium wines that do very well in blind tastings and have great followings all over the globe. As we will see, Concha y Toro (CYT) exports to 135 countries and has become the third largest winemaker in the world and the largest in South America.

The various micro-climates are fascinating. Deserts, high elevation, extremely cold wind from the Pacific Ocean, the pure water from the Andes run-off, among other characteristics of different sectors, make Chile a diverse and productive center for many different styles of wine. In the following chapter we will examine each area individually from the winemaking point of view. Below we will look at some cultural and historical aspects.

The North, as we have mentioned, is a desert. The so-called Valley of the Moon in the Atacama desert is a subject of interest, as it looks so much like the moon. There are stories, believed by many locals, that the astronauts took pictures in the Chilean desert that they were unable to take on the real moon. Regardless, the resemblance is eerie, to say the least. In today's wine world, the desert land is slowly being used for vineyard plantations and the results are magnificent. On the Eastern side there a many volcanoes overlooking the area, many of which are still active. To the West is the Cordillera de Sal, a mountain range dominated by salt mines. This fascinating area was ruled by the Incans from 1450 until the invasion of the Spaniards some 100 years later.

Just south of the Atacama Desert, Elqui Valley is an oasis that is quickly developing into an extremely attractive wine growing area. Crystal clear skies offer star filled nights and sun drenched days. With elevations of 6500 feet above sea level, Elqui is Chile's highest and northernmost wine area. A dense fog, the Camanchaca, creeps up daily and blankets the vineyards with cool air and moisture. Near the coast the temperatures are quite low, getting warmer inland. New projects include terraces in the Andes reaching 6500 feet above sea level. The area is a tourist attraction and the vineyards will have a heavy amount of visitors in future years. Syrah has become the grape of choice as it responds so well to the extremes of the valley area, but Cabernet is still predominant with 40% of the production.

Limari and Choapa Valleys just to the South are known for their fruit growing and archaeological digs, but have been producing wines since the 1990's. Today there are some 15 vineyards, some producing excellent wines. The very dry and pest-free environment is ideal for organic, biodynamic winegrowing. The mineral deposits that characterize the valley help give character to the crisp white wines found here. Choapa valley produces Syrah. The high acidity and low pH found here presents interesting prospects for future vineyards. What is called the Coquimbo region is made up of the latter three valleys and is one of the Denomination of Origin (D.O.) areas. Around one third of the production is Cabernet Sauvignon.

The Aconcagua Region goes up to the enormous Central Valley and includes areas that begin as close to the beach as 2 miles and stretch to the Andes Mountains. Aconcagua is the name of the highest mountain in the Andes, 23,000 feet above sea level. Many of the best organic vineyards are found here and in Casablanca Valley. Cabernet Sauvignon and Carmenere thrive here. To the west is the fertile Casablanca Valley, beginning just off the Ocean. This area has fascinating micro-climates that allow the temperature during the day to reach 90 F degrees and fall at night to 42 F. The cold, moist winds come off the Ocean in the evenings through the early morning, sometimes creating dark fog over the vineyards which disappear around noon, allowing the summer sunlight to cover the land. These abrupt alterations require very experienced and talented winemakers to turn these changes into advantages for growing grapes. The vineyards near the ocean are famous for their white and pinot noir wines.

Maipo Valley houses many of the traditional premium vineyards of the country and is home to Santiago, the capital city. Cabernet Sauvignon makes up some 60% of the plantations in the area.

Rapel/Cachapoal Valley is 100 km south of Santiago and is one of the principal agricultural centers of Chile. 90% of the wine are red varietals, with proximity to the Andes being the strongest area. Large temperature variations and poor soil make for great wines, as counter intuitive as that may seem! The Peumo sector produces some of the best Carmenere in the country. Rapel is also the Rodeo capital; many of the wineries here have tours on horses that go up part of the Andes mountains for meals and wine tastings.

Rapel/Colchagua Valley has a warm climate and produces great red wines, principally Carmenere and Cabs. Apalta, now considered the Bordeaux of Chile, is the center of this area. The town of Santa Cruz is becoming a tourist mecca for wine lovers, with a working tourist winery, a large hotel and a casino.

Curico Valley is characterized by the Coastal range of mountains, which with the Andes compose a true valley. The cool air makes this area the prime producer of Sauvignon Blanc in Chile. Dormant volcanoes dominate the Eastern ridge of the Andes. Waterfalls and beautiful Lake Vichuquen make this valley a visual paradise and a significant tourist attraction.

Maule Valley dates back centuries and is Chile's largest wine region. Many small independent vineyards dot the valley, with Carmenere being one of the outstanding grapes produced.

Itata Valley is to the South of Maule and has Concepcion as its major port city. The latter is where the first missionaries came with vines to plant. Characterized by great skiing and hot springs in the Andes, Itata is quickly becoming a tourist mecca.

Bio Bio and Malleco Valleys are remote paradises with reduced summer seasons. The courageous winemakers fight cold and short seasons to make interesting wines, principally whites. Frost is a constant enemy of fine wines.

The significance of these regions is that Chilean law requires that 75% of the grapes be from a particular region in order to use the region as identification. Hence, to be a Casablanca Pinot Noir, 75% of the grapes must be certified to have its origin in that Valley. Similarly, to be denominated something other than a blend, at least 80% must be of the dominant grape. Exported wine, which is some 3/4 of the wine produced in Chile, voluntarily use the international standard of 85%.

Today, Chile is the fourth largest exporter of wines to the U.S. In 1995, there were 12 wineries in Chile; today there are over 80.

In 1996, Chile exported 100,000 cases to the U.S.; today over 5 million

In 1985, there were 30 acres of Chardonnay planted; today over 15,000 acres.

Cabernet Sauvignon is the largest planted grape in Chile with over 40% of the acreage planted.

Concha y Toro is the oldest of the present wineries, having been founded in 1888. Although their Maipo vineyard is verdant today, it originally was in the midst of a semi-desert, hours from Santiago by horse. Don Melchor Concha y Toro married Emiliana, whose father, a very rich industrialist, made the irrigation project to bring water from the government irrigation system, developed from the Incan times, to their then vacation land, And so Concha y Toro soon had its oasis to initiate its winery. Today, CYT is the largest wine company in South America and one of the largest in the world. It is the only one listed on the New York Stock Exchange. Emiliana is a fascinating independent subsidiary and the largest producer of organic and biodynamic wines in Chile.

We will now examine individually Chile's best wineries. As a reminder, our scoring rating does not evaluate wines that are not at least rated very-good. Therefore, the reader will not be subjected to negative reviews, as all the wines in this book are from very good, to outstanding, to great.

ALMAVIVA

In 1997, the Lafitte Rothschild group joined with Concha y Toro to make a superb, Bordeaux styled wine and Almaviva was born. The name is not really Spanish as it comes from a play written in the 18th century by Beaumarchais, which later became the opera, The Marriage of Figaro. Its hero was Count Almaviva, Almaviva coming from the Latin meaning a live soul. Interestingly, the name Almaviva is handwritten just as Beaumarchais wrote it himself on the cover of his manuscript.

The label, meanwhile, comes from designs symbolizing the cosmos and earth in the Mapuche Indian tradition. The Indians painted these designs on their ritual drums, called kultruns.

The vineyard calls Almaviva a Primer Orden, equivalent in Spanish to Premier Cru in French, or something like Highest level, or First Growth, as we call the best eight French wines. To be so, it must be made from a single vineyard and the winery and winemaker and his technical team must be dedicated to the making of only that one wine, in this case Almaviva.

The winery is located on 85 hectares in the Maipo Valley in a subsection named Puente Alto or high point. The climate is characterized by hot summer days and cold summer nights, rainy winters, and a stony, clay like soil. The irrigation is a modern drip system, computer controlled, that services the vines with an ideal amount of water year round. Throughout the winery, there are displays of native artifacts and designs of the Mapuche tribe.

Almaviva is a blend of predominantly Cabernet Sauvignon combined with Carmenere and Cabernet Franc. In my opinion, it is the finest wine produced in Chile, using a true combination of the best Bordeaux grapes cultivated over centuries in the tropical Chilean climate, thereby producing a tropical, full-bodied taste with the subtly and finesse of the best French winemaking. A work of art!

Visits by appointment only. Very close to Santiago.
info@almavivawinery.com

ALMAVIVA 2007

COLOR   Intense Violet
AROMA   Enticing subtle bouquet of red berries
BODY   Full, super structured, dense; finest blending, mild oak
PALATE   Round, Velvety smooth, but tropical fruits prevail; Elegant
FINISH   Long, languid, incredibly delicious

GREAT

64% Cab, 28% Carmenere, 7% Cab Franc, 1% Merlot, 18 months in new French oak. Except for the Merlot, the grapes were picked in the third week of May, allowing for an extraordinary amount of hang time. The result is superb. A tropical grand cru, just as promised. 12th vintage and maybe the best. I must emphasize that although the style is French, the taste is Chilean, individualistic, and superb. It is impossible to exaggerate how terrific this wine is. I was fortunate to retaste Almaviva at The Wine Spectator Wine Experience. I compared it head to head with Chateau Margaux, Chateau Lafitte and Cheval Blanc, among others. Almaviva is in the same class. This is one to buy, drink now, and keep for the future to celebrate an important family event. Very difficult to beat! A work of art. $95

CASA SILVA

The oldest winery in Colchagua Valley, Casa Silva is an example of taking the rich history of wine-making in Chile and combining it with cutting edge technology to produce outstanding wines in a beautiful, culturally rich setting. Founded in 1892 by Emile Bouchon, a French émigré, Casa Silva became the most important winery in Colchagua Valley and grew through the generations. Bouchon's granddaughter married Jorge Silva and eventually the winery took the Silva name.

In 1977, the fourth generation of family expanded the growth of the bulk wine business. Mario Pablo Silva, today's President and fifth generation of family management, convinced his father to switch from the mass production of basic wine to premium quality and, in 1997, the present style of Casa Silva began to take form. Today, Mario and his brothers manage the winery with a talented young staff.

Some five years ago, on a trip to Brazil, I had the pleasure of tasting my first Carmenere wine, which was a Casa Silva Carmenere Reserva. I remember that evening fondly and it was an extra pleasure to visit the historical winery and see first hand where it was produced.

The winery is large and possesses many interesting cultural and artistic projects that make it a true Chilean center for sports and the arts. Along with soccer, Chile possesses a passion for polo and rodeo. Casa Silva has an equestrian center in a magnificent group of preserved buildings, which include a polo field, a rodeo pitch, and a significant equestrian club with stables of horses for classes and riding. Horse-drawn carriage rides are one of the tours available to visitors. As it happens, Rodeo is one of the top three sports in Chile and is very popular across all levels of society. Casa Silva is the rodeo center for the Colchagua Valley.

Casa Silva's hotel and restaurant are high quality locations, staffed by attentive workers and one could use the hotel as a base for seeing the many wineries in the vicinity. The hotel is a converted home for the estate and houses 7 beautiful, large rooms. The restaurant has a wonderful Chilean menu and is happily non smoking. The beautiful bar downstairs, with an excellent wine tasting menu, allows smokers. A large selection of Cuban cigars are available. Both overlook the barrel cellar creating a charming atmosphere for an evening out. The building housing all of the latter attractions dates from the 19th century and is fully preserved. The vineyard has the infra-structure for the visitor to experience an informative wine tour, catch a rodeo and/or polo match, take a buggy ride or horse back tour, or just chill out in a magnificent setting. The wine shop offers the total production of the winery at accessible prices, as well as a broad line of souvenirs. Reservations essential. www.casasilva.cl; casasilva@casasilva.cl

CASA SILVA SAUVIGNON BLANC RESERVA 2009

COLOR   Pale Yellow
AROMA   Complex. Inviting bouquet of citrus and minerals
BODY   Round, Full, Sea Air notes over smooth citrus, Delicious
PALATE   Dry, mineral and citrus, smooth, great for sushi or thai food
FINISH   Smooth, long, wonderfully refreshing

OUTSTANDING
100% Sauvignon Blanc, 10,000 cases, from vineyards 3-4 miles from Pacific Ocean, very strong influence of sea, $14

CASA SILVA SAUVIGNON GRIS 2009

COLOR   Pale Yellow
AROMA   Wonderful bouquet of citrus,/minerals
BODY   Full, Round, lots of fruit
PALATE   Complex, Opulent, interesting, very rewarding,
FINISH   Smooth with citrus finish, mild acidity, no bitterness; long

OUTSTANDING
100% Colchagua Valley, from vines planted in 1912, single vineyard, 100% Sauvignon Gris, original and rewarding wine; $19

CASA SILVA CHARDONNAY ANGOSTURA GRAN RESERVA 2008

COLOR   Light Maize
AROMA   Inviting blend of citrus and minerals
BODY   Straight forward, not complex, tropical fruits, well balanced
PALATE   Smooth, keeps improving with each taste, Easy
FINISH   Smooth, Refreshing

VERY GOOD TO OUTSTANDING
100% Chardonnay, 30% in oak for 6 months, $20

CASA SILVA QUINTA GENERACION 2007

COLOR   Yellow

AROMA   Enticing spices and oak muted fruits, Chablis-like

BODY   Full, Complex, lots of minerals, Pears, Fruits, buttery rich

PALATE   Round, Smooth, Structured, Terrific Complex. Integrated oak tones

FINISH   Opulent, Long, Refreshing and Crisp, Can drink with or without food

GREAT

even mix of Sauvignon Gris, Viognier, Chardonnay, 2/3 oak, Like most of the Casa Silva whites, the taste is complex and original, terrific wine, $27

CASA SILVA CAMENERE RESERVA 2008

COLOR   Deep Fuchsia

AROMA   Inviting Bouquet of Blackberries

BODY   Big, Full, Very structured; needs lots of time to breathe, dense

PALATE   Round, Very complex, lots of spices complement the fruits

FINISH   Smooth, very long, Delicious

OUTSTANDING

100% Carmenere, Blended from different estates of the winery, especially Los Lingues e Lolo, half in oak 6 months, 20,000 cases, $13

CASA SILVA MERLOT ANGOSTURA GRAN RESERVA 2007

COLOR   Intense Violet

AROMA   Alluring Fruit Bouquet, Muted and French Style

BODY   Full, Complex, Oak muting of Big Fruits

PALATE   Smooth and complex, very rewarding

FINISH   Long and Smooth,

OUTSTANDING TO GREAT

100% Merlot, 80% in oak for 10 months, $19

CASA SILVA CARMENERE LOS LINGUES GRAN RESERVA 2007

COLOR   Deep Purple
AROMA   Very Complex and inviting, Promises a lot—
       Fruits/Pepper
BODY   Smooth, Full, Well Structured, Fabulous
PALATE   Velvety Smooth, Wonderfully Complex, Layers of
       Fruit
FINISH   Very Long, Smooth,

GREAT

100% Carmenere, single vineyard from Los Lingues, 11 months in oak, Great buy at $20

CASA SILVA CABERNET SAUVIGNON LOS LINGUES GRAN RESERVA 2007

COLOR   Deep Purple, Almost Black
AROMA   Wonderful Bouquet of Black Fruit
BODY   Full, Structured, Balanced, Complex blend of
       Fruits and Minerals
PALATE   Rewarding taste of Fruits, supported by spices
       and minerals
FINISH   Smooth as silk, long and languid end

OUTSTANDING TO GREAT

100% Cab, single vineyard, 11 months in oak, half new, for 90% of the grapes; $20

CASA SILVA PETIT VERDOT GRAN RESERVA 2007

COLOR   Dark Purple
AROMA   Mild bouquet of Red Fruit and pepper
BODY   Medium, Round, Very Smooth, Mild Tannins
PALATE   Concentrated, Smooth, Elegant, Layers of
       different dark fruits dominate
FINISH   Long, delicious, happy ending

OUTSTANDING TO GREAT

100% Petit Verdot, 2 vineyards, 11 months in French oak, $20

CASA SILVA QUINTA GENERACION RED 2005

COLOR   Very Intense Violet
AROMA   Soft but complex bouquet of layers of dark fruit, muted by oak
BODY   Full, Complex, Masculine, Lots of Dark Fruit, Peppers, Herbs
PALATE Excellent structure, Round and Smooth. Very special, sensuous
FINISH   Velvety smooth, very long end, almost languishing
GREAT
blend of 45% Carmenere, rest Syrah, Cab, and Petit Verdot. 100% in oak for 1 year, 2500 cases, $28

CASA SILVA MICROTERROIR DE LOS LINGUES CARMENERE 2006

COLOR   Intense Violet
AROMA   Alluring Layered Bouquet of Fruits, Herbs and Peppers
BODY   Full, Complex, Interesting and Lovely
PALATE Round, Well Structured and Balanced, Fruits/Peppers/Spices/Herbs
FINISH   Silky Smooth, Very Long
GREAT
takes wine to a totally higher level, 100% Carmenere, taken from 11 micro plots, Super special selection, hand picked, double elimination, $45

CASA SILVA ALTURA 2004

COLOR   Almost Black
AROMA   Extremely inviting with big smooth waifs of Black Berry
BODY   Full, Delicious, Very Round and well structured
PALATE Intense and Elegant; Very expressive; layers of Grapes
FINISH   Smooth as velvet, long, harmonious and Sensual
GREAT
Icon wine, 50% Carmenere, 33$ Cab, rest Petit Verdot, 700 cases, Blind taste it against your favorite Bordeaux, $65

CONCHA Y TORO

Concha Y Toro is a superstar producer of exceptionally high quality wines. True, Concha y Toro is one of the largest wine producers in the world and by far the largest in Latin America. With almost $600 million in sales and over 26 million cases sold a year, the company is known for bulk wine that can be bought for a very low price.

Let it be known, however, that while the bulk wines will continue to sell successfully and very profitably, CYT is leading the way, along with many other Chilean wineries, in producing high quality, well-priced premium brands consumed at the best tables worldwide. All will be fully described herein.

Concha y Toro celebrated 126 years of winemaking in 2009 and is riding the crest of its relatively new strategy of emphasizing premium wines, which happens to give a higher profit margin, albeit a smaller scale of production.

One of its subsidiaries, a joint venture with Baron Phillippe de Rothschild, Almaviva, for years has produced superb, French Bordeaux-like wines. CYT's premium wines, led by Terrunyo, are off the charts. The Carmenere on all levels, but particularly all of the Terrunyos, are world class and excellent values. Their relatively unknown quality, as with so many other wineries, is the *raison d'etre* of this book. The world has to discover these fabulous wines!

CYT first exported in 1933 to Holland. Today, the company exports about 93% of its wine production. Concha y Toro products can be found in 136 different countries.

Concha y Toro invested $74 million in 2008 alone in expanding its production and now has over 8,000 hectares planted in the wine area of Chile. Still, its average export price per case is around $24 so it can be concluded that inexpensive wines still dominate its overall production.

One of the most surprising aspects of the business is its store at the headquarters in Maipo. This vineyard is the most popular tourist attraction in the country, receiving approximately 100,000 visitors a year. Its well-laid-out store stocks most of its wine products.

The store's sales exceed the sales total to a number of the countries to which they export. Next to the store and tasting rooms is a wonderful, rustic restaurant, serving traditional Chilean fare at very reasonable prices. This is a tremendous company and we will now focus on the great wines it produces.
www.vinoscyt.com

TERRUNYO SAUVIGNON BLANC 2008

COLOR Clear lemon maize
AROMA Mild mineral and citrus bouquet, certain touch of flowers
BODY Some complexity, lots of fruit, not sweet, flowers abound
PALATE Smooth, delicious, round, mineral overtones
FINISH Smooth and languid

OUTSTANDING
100% Casablanca Valley, Terrunyo wines are one of the super-premium brands produced by CYT. Around $25

TERRUNYO AMELIA CHARDONNAY EL TRIANGULO VINEYARD 2007

COLOR Pale maize
AROMA Fabulous inviting bouquet of minerals and muted pears
BODY Full, round, superb, Chablis-like style; low acidity
PALATE Round fruity taste, smooth, elegant, sophisticated
FINISH Full and ultra smooth; long lasting, wonderful

GREAT
9 months in oak, mainly Casablanca Valley, 5% from Limari, only 500 cases, but production to increase; Chardonnay cannot get much better than this. Put it up in a blind tasting against Burgundy!! Ignacio Recabarren is the winemaker for Terrunyo; this Chard puts him up there among Chile's stars! $35

TERRUNYO CARMENERE 2002/2004

COLOR Very Intense violet, almost black
AROMA Full, very inviting; intense, Bordeaux style
BODY Big, muscular, very smooth, round flow of dark berries/spices
PALATE Velvet dark berry, minerality, spices, herbs, complex, superb
FINISH Silky smooth, long lasting, heavenly delicious

GREAT
Ready right now, 90% Carmenere, 7% Cab, also Petit Verdot and Cab Franc, blend changes depending on crop production, but quality is just phenomenal. Very late harvest; 2009 Malbec was picked at the end of May. The complexity

of the Carmenere is dominant but the supporting grapes give structure and depth. Any serious wine lover should find this wine at any price. It is laughable to omit this wine from any "TOP" list. A steal at only $45

TERRUNYO CABERNET SAUVIGNON 2007

COLOR   Purple/black
AROMA   Super-inviting mix of dark fruits and
           minerals
BODY   Full, lots of fruits and minerals
PALATE   Round, wonderful, strong and smooth
FINISH   Very long and smooth, delicious

OUTSTANDING TO GREAT
16 months in oak, 600 cases, 3% Cab Franc, $40

MARQUES DE CASA CONCHA MERLOT 2007

COLOR   Purple, almost black
AROMA   Terrific, round and inviting
BODY   Medium to full, elegant,
PALATE   Muted fruits, very Bordeaux-like, round
FINISH   Smooth and long lasting, very sensual

OUTSTANDING TO GREAT
100% Merlot, vineyard block next to Almaviva, very special Incredible value at $20. The whole line of Marques de Casa Concha is exceptional in quality and value. The Carmenere, Syrah and Merlot are superb wines, as are the Chardonnay and Sauvignon Blanc.

TERRUNYO CARMIN DE PEUMO CARMENERE 2005

COLOR   Intense violet
AROMA   Alluring bouquet of blackberries
BODY   Full, very round; exquisite
PALATE   Smooth, complex, layers of berries, spices
FINISH   Very long, languid, sensual, silky smooth

GREAT
D.O. Peumo, a superb vineyard in Cachopoal Valley, harvested May 16 (very late) adding longer hang time for the full taste of the Carmenere grape, supported by some Cabernet Sauvignon and Cabernet Franc, 18 months in new French oak, additional year in bottle aging, MUST BREATHE 40 minutes to be appreciated, A complex wine that deserves patience before imbibing! $100

DON MELCHOR 2006

COLOR   Deep purple (older vintages lighter with age)

AROMA   Very Inviting, big and round, muted fruits, Bordeaux-like

BODY   Elegant, delicate fruits, very round, very special

PALATE   Sophisticated, smooth, silky, soft fruits, mild minerals

FINISH   Elegant, smooth, languid and long lasting

GREAT

Chile's first true Icon, began in 1987, it ages but not sure if it gets better – the 1991 is lighter in color and body, still lovely, but weaker than 2006; originally 100% Cab, 2006 has 4% Cab Franc, 14 months in months in oak, 65% in first-use oak, from vineyard of 114 acres, super selective picking, 20,000 cases; $80

ECHEVERRIA

Located exactly at the 35th parallel, at the foothills of the Andes Mountains, and within a short distance from the Pacific Ocean in Curico, Echeverria is a family winery, headed by Roberto Echeverria, in which all of the important positions are held by family members.

Their wines are exported to 40 countries. Echeverria produces 120,000 cases per annum and have four styles of wine categories. Roberto is a Phd from Cornell University and a former economist at the World Bank. The introductory Classics are quality, low priced wines with 6 individual varietals. Echeverria welcomes visitors with reservations made prior to visit. www.echewine.com

ECHEVERRIA SAUVIGNON BLANC RESERVA 2009

COLOR   Pale Yellow
AROMA   Inviting bouquet of flowers and minerals, citrus notes
BODY   Very Round, full grapefruit and lime;
PALATE   Citrus, flowers and minerals blended well, fresh and crisp
FINISH   Smooth, long, ideal for grilled shrimp

OUTSTANDING
100% Sauvignon Blanc, 100% hand picked, single vineyard, Molina, $15

ECHEVERRIA MERLOT RESERVA, 2006

COLOR   Violet
AROMA   Inviting; Berry bouquet
BODY   Full, Round, Lots of cassis berry
PALATE   Muted Berry tones with very mild spice, some mineral notes
FINISH   Smooth

OUTSTANDING
100% Merlot, hand picked, aged 12 months in oak, single vineyard, Molina, $15

ECHEVERRIA CABERNET SAUVIGNON RESERVA 2006

COLOR   Crimson
AROMA   Very inviting, bouquet of berries, minerals and spices
BODY   Full, Round, Lots of fruit
PALATE   Smooth, Easy, Red and Black berries dominate

FINISH   Smooth, long and easy

VERY GOOD TO OUTSTANDING
Single vineyard, 12 months in oak, hand picked, 100% Cab, $15

ECHEVERRIA CARMENERE RESERVA 2007

COLOR   Deep Violet

AROMA   Very enticing bouquet of red and black berries, lots of spices

BODY   Big, Full, Round, Strong sense of complex berries/spices

PALATE   Delicious, Very Big but very smooth, one of my favorites

FINISH   Very smooth, long and pleasurable

OUTSTANDING TO GREAT
100% Carmenere, a splendid wine that I personally have been drinking for many years; single vineyard, 10 months in French oak, Central Valley, old vines, $15

ECHEVERRIA FOUNDER'S SELECTION 2005

COLOR   Intense Violet

AROMA   Alluring Red berry bouquet

BODY   Smooth, straightforward, Red berry, some cassis tones

PALATE   Round, Full, Smooth, not complex

FINISH   Smooth, very easy

OUTSTANDING
100% Cab, from Central Valley old vines, 24 months in oak, hand selected, low yield, $39

SPECIAL SELECTION LATE HARVEST SAUVIGNON BLANC 2005

COLOR   Light Gold

AROMA   Inviting bouquet of Peaches, Honey, assemblage of other fruits

BODY   Wonderful, sweet fruity wine for after dinner or with dessert

PALATE   Full, Round, delicious Fruits, Very Elegant

FINISH   Smooth, sweet, Very enjoyable, terrific after meats

OUTSTANDING

100% Sauvignon Blanc, single vineyard, 100% hand picked in Winter; Moderately aged in French oak; serve around 45 degrees F; $25

EMILIANA

Vinedos Emiliana was founded in 1986. The name originates from Concha Y Toro's founder's wife and is named in her honor. Emiliana is a totally independent winery, with very specific principles, including producing wines organically and bio-dynamically. Their motto is "Quality Born in our Vineyards".

The winery owns 1550 hectares of planted vineyards, from some of the best areas of Chile. In 2001, the winery won the ISO 14.001 certification. The management is dedicated to respecting the environment and 1998 began the organic development of their wines, Emiliana Organico, which, they feel, preserves the terroir in the most natural fashion.

Today, the Natura and Novas wines are organically made. Natura is the largest non-U.S. organically produced line of wines in the world. Coyam and G are made bio-dynamically. All are certified as such. Headquartered in the heart of Colchagua Valley, Emiliana produces 300,000 cases of wine per annum. The company is a very serious and dedicated affair, with special wines and a beautiful set of vineyards.

Fernando Pavon is the very serious winery manager who has put together a youthful, dedicated staff. Rafael and Jose Guilisasti are the principal directors. Antonio Bravo is the brilliant head winemaker. Their wines are exported to 40 countries, the principle destination being the U.S. Their varietal lines of Natura are very enjoyable.

Emiliana is one of the most visited vineyards in Chile and is extremely tourist friendly, with a beautiful store and wine tasting areas.

Personal Note: I applaud the efforts of the directorate of Emiliana to respect the environment and make organic and bio-dynamic wines. These wines are terrific wines by any level of rating. The Emiliana vineyards in Casablanca Valley set an example for the entire world that great wines can be produced by such methods. The animals and the natural environment preserved on the large plantation lend another dimension to the pleasure of producing truly sensational wines. wineshop@emiliana.cl; fpavon@emiliana.cl; www.emiliana.cl

EMILIANA SAUVIGNON BLANC NOVAS LIMITED EDITION 2009

COLOR	Clear Yellow
AROMA	Wonderful Bouquet of Citrus and Flowers; Inviting
BODY	Lovely in the Mouth, Light, refreshing; Muted Citrus/Minerals
PALATE	Grapefruit stands out; soft Tropical touches, mineral hints
FINISH	Terrific citrus taste, with background of flowers

Emiliana

NOVAS

Limited Selection

SAUVIGNON BLANC

MADE WITH ORGANICALLY GROWN GRAPES

VERY GOOD
1500 cases, organic, 100% Casablanca Vally, $15

EMIILANA CHARDONNAY NOVAS 2008 LIMITED EDITION

COLOR   Light Maize
AROMA   Fruity with floral hints
BODY   Light, smooth; mix of fruits, minerals/flowers, touch of vanilla
PALATE Fresh, Very tasty, dry, spices embedded in citrus
FINISH Smooth, light Tropical; very refreshing

VERY GOOD
95% Chard, 5% Viognier, 50% in oak fermentation; $15

EMILIANA CHARDONNAY VIOGNIER NOVAS 2007

COLOR   Pale Yellow
AROMA   Invitingly complex; mineral overtones, fruit, flowers abound
BODY   Slight sweetness, Tropical, Herbs, fruits and flowers multiply
PALATE Full, round, sweetly flowery, touches of herbs, complex
FINISH Smooth and delicious, wonderful blend of flavors

OUTSTANDING
65% Chardonnay, 35% Viognier, 6 months in French oak, additional 6 months in bottles; The effect of this mix of grapes is to make a most delicious and unusual blend of flavors and aromas, all of which work superbly. $25

EMILIANA PINOT NOIR RESERVA ESPECIAL 2007

COLOR   Purple
AROMA   Floral and Fruity—very inviting
BODY   Smooth, light, easy to drink, integrated spicy oak
PALATE Round, tropical fruits abound, well balanced, elegant
FINISH Flowing smoothly; delicious, terrific for couples

OUTSTANDING
100% from Casablanca, 8 months in French oak, 8 months in bottle, 1st vintage, destined for U.S. market; $25

EMILIANA CARMENERE NATURA 2008

COLOR   Intense Violet
AROMA Round bouquet of Dark berries and spices; inviting
BODY   Full, still young, lots of spices mixed with fruits; complex
PALATE Round, spice, berries. Minerals, dense
FINISH Smooth and delicious, excellent length

OUTSTANDING
100% Carmenere from Colchagua Valley, though a mid level varietal, this wine is big and with age will be great; $14

EMILIANA NOVAS LIMITED SELECT 2007

COLOR   Intense Violet
AROMA Round, inviting bouquet of berries and spices; promises a lot
BODY   Full and Round, Big and firm, terrific
PALATE Smooth, the Cab softens the taste, lots of fruits/spice overtones
FINISH Smooth and delicious

OUTSTANDING TO GREAT
12,000 Cases; 54% Carmenere, 46% Cab, 100% aged for 8 months in French oak, terrific effort, will improve even more with age; $25

EMILIANA NOVAS CABERNET SAUVIGNON-MERLOT 2006

COLOR   Deep Purple
AROMA Round and fruity, very inviting
BODY   Full, Lots of Fruit, smooth and Round
PALATE Merlot grape rounds off taste, very smooth, mild fruits
FINISH Smooth, delicious

OUTSTANDING
54% Cab, 46% Merlot, Central Valley vineyards, $15

EMILIANA NOVAS SYRAH 2005

COLOR   Intense Purple, almost black
AROMA Terrific bouquet, French styled, muted fruits

BODY   Full, mild oak finish on big fruits;
PALATE   Smooth, Round Structured and serious, yet sensual
FINISH   Smooth, easy

GREAT

a wonderful Syrah, very special, small production, 100% Syrah, winemaker's selection, only 2nd vintage, 1 year in oak barrels, 1 year in bottle, $20, if you find it, buy it!!

COYAM SUPER PREMIUM RESERVE

COLOR   Deep Purple
AROMA   Big, strong and appealing; lots of fruits and
         minerals
BODY   Full, Round, Blend of many fruits and spices,
         Complex
PALATE   Muscular, big, needs aging and time but is
         wonderful already
FINISH   Silky smooth, but very distinctive and original

GREAT

Blend of Berries, Syrah, Merlot, Cab, Carmenere, touch of Malbec; Blend changes every year depending on yield and taste; Very original and complex, needs lots of time to breathe and will age very well; Coyam means oak in the Mapuche language, this tribe being the original inhabitants of what is now Chile. Ancient Oak trees surround the vineyards in Casablanca. Along with Ge, Coyam is perhaps the best Organic, biodynamic wine ever made; $40

EMILIANA Ge

COLOR   Intense Purple
AROMA   Very smoky, woody, muted berries, very
         inviting
BODY   Full, very big, muted tastes of fruit, herbs,
         spices, minerals
PALATE   Smooth, round, very intense, Delicious, Great
         Structure
FINISH   Smooth as silk, round, full, languishing taste

GREAT

Icon of the winery, 55% Syrah, 15% each of Cab, Carmenere, Merlot. Blend varies from year to year. Ge stands for earth in Greek. (As in Geology) This biodynamic, organic wine is the expression of terroir that Emiliana wants to present to the world; $80

ERRAZURIZ

Vina Errazuriz was founded in 1870 by Don Maximiano Errazuriz in the Aconcagua Valley, 100 kilometers North of Santiago. The vineyards were planted in barren land with vines brought from Europe. A long history of family run vineyards was started and today his descendant, the sixth generation to direct the winery, Eduardo Chadwick, has modernized the entire operation and opened new markets with superb, award winning wines. With vineyards in Curico and Casablanca having been added, Errazuriz produces estate made wines with control from planting to winemaking, using the most natural techniques.

The wines are characterized by complexity and elegance. Francisco Baettig is the head winemaker and has led the winery since 2003, after establishing a very impressive curricula. Errazuriz has won numerous awards worldwide in blind tasting against France's first growths.

The Errazuriz family is one of the most traditional in Chile and has produced 4 Presidents, 2 Archbishops of the Catholic Church in Santiago, and numerous diplomats and entrepeneurs. Maximiano himself, married the daughter of the richest man in Chile and went on to be his partner in Copper mines and the gas company that made the first streetlights in the country. At one point, the Copper company produced 1/3 of the world's copper production. Don Maximiano had a fascinating life, serving as a senator of the republic and a diplomat in the U.S. His home in Santiago serves as the Brazilian Embassy today.

The winery has an estate entry-level group of wines that are very good., especially the Carmenere. Errazuriz is extremely tourist friendly with 1 and 2 hour tours. There is an outstanding wine tasting room and shop. Reservations essential. cellardoor@errazuriz.cl; www.errazuriz.com

ERRAZURIZ CHARDONNAY WILD FERMENT 2008

COLOR   Pale Yellow
AROMA   Enticing bouquet of citric and sweet fruits
BODY   Medium, refreshing taste of pear and
        grapefruit
PALATE Round, lots of character, mild acidity, layers of
        fruit
FINISH Smooth, long, elegant

OUTSTANDING
Lovely in the mouth with embedded citrus, Barrel Fermented, 21% in new French oak for 10 months adds complexity, 100% Chardonnay, from La Escultura Estate in Casablanca, $20

DON MAXIMIANO SINGLE VINEYARD ESTATE CARMENERE 2007

COLOR   Intense Violet
AROMA   Complex Bouquet of Black Fruits and Spices
BODY   Full, wonderful mix of Dark Fruit, minerals and spices
PALATE   Round, Dense, Complex: layers of fruits, peppers, cinnamon
FINISH   Very long and smooth, delicious

OUTSTANDING
1 Year in new oak, 3% Shiraz, rest Carmenere, all from Aconchagua Estate, Lush and elegant, a great value at $20

ERRAZURIZ MAX RESERVA SHIRAZ 2005

COLOR   Intense Purple
AROMA   Smoky Inviting Bouquet of Berries
BODY   Full, Big Blackberry and Plum muted by the chocolaty oak
PALATE   Round and dense; well-structured layers of berries
FINISH   Smooth and long—languishingly persistent

OUTSTANDING
100% Shiraz, from original Aconcagua estate, 1 year in oak, 48% new, low yield and carefully hand-picked, $20

ERRAZURIZ VINEDO CHADWICK 2007

COLOR   Deep Purple
AROMA   Inviting Bouquet of Black Cherries and Blackberries
BODY   Full, very well-structured, dense
PALATE   Round, Multi layered berries pouring in; Great depth
FINISH   Smooth as silk, long and rewarding—a real pleasure

GREAT
800 cases, from Maipu Valley vineyard, sustainable agricultural practices; 19 months in new French oak; a superb wine, can be compared to the best Bordeaux wine, $100

ERRAZURIZ LATE HARVEST SAUVIGNON BLANC 2007

COLOR   Golden hues over a deep Maize

AROMA   Enticing bouquet of apricots and honey

BODY   Full, dense, smooth, lots of sweet fruits, delicious

PALATE   Round, persuasive apricots, pears, raisins, honey abound

FINISH   Long, sensuous and wonderfully delicious

OUTSTANDING

85% Sauvignon Blanc, 15% Gewurztraminer, delicious dessert wine, smooth and rewarding, single vineyard from Casablanca Valley, fermented in stainless steel, but for 11% which is fermented in French oak barrels, which gives greater texture and volume. $12

LAPOSTOLLE

One of the fascinating stories of modern Chilean wine history, Lapostolle characterizes itself as the marriage of French know-how and Chile's perfect wine growing conditions. The latter includes a mild climate cooled by ocean breezes, disease free land and winter only rainfall. Housed in the heart of Apalta, Chile's "Bordeaux", Lapostolle is a magnificent, modern museum to taste, class and sophistication. The building itself, reminds one of a Guggenheim Museum in mid-town New York. Breathtaking in design, shadowy and dramatic, with granite walls and a huge, central staircase, the modern architecture exploits nature and the wine making process for incredible angles and views of what is normally routine procedures of making wine.

Founded in 1994 by Alexandra Marnier Lapostolle and her husband Cyril, the former the heir to the Marnier Beverage Company of France, makers of inter alia, Grand Marnier, Lapostolle has become an iconic producer of fabulous wine, its flagship wine, Clos Apalta winning many of the important International awards. Though best know for Grand Marnier, the French parent makes many other products, most especially Chateau de Sancerre.

The famed French consultant Michel Rolland was the brains behind these great brands that have been developed on some of the richest vineyards in the country. With 925 acres planted on their own property and another 500 under contract, Lapostolle produces 200,000 cases of wine from 7 different grapes. The product is exported to over 70 countries.

The vinicultural staff are young, enthusiastic and dedicated. Andrea Leon, a winemaker and communications director, is extremely knowledgeable and helpful in explaining the process used at Casa Lapostolle. There are 3 vineyards, the home at Apalta, La Kuras in Cachapoal Valley, for Sauvignon Blanc and Syrah, and Atalayas Vineyard in Casablanca Valley for Chardonnay.

The property has a sexy 4 room hotel which has just been refurbished, a wonderful restaurant and beautiful tasting rooms. Tours are possible with reservations. www.casalapostolle.com; info@lapostolle.com; www.lapostolle.com. residence@lapostolle.com

LAPOSTOLLE CASA SAUVIGNON BLANC 2009

COLOR   Pale Yellow
AROMA   Notes of sweet fruit, flowers and minerality
BODY   Full, soft flavors of lychee, touches of minerals
PALATE   Velvety fruit, mild acidity, Refreshing, crisp
FINISH   Smooth, Special taste, Crisp

VERY GOOD TO OUTSTANDING
92% Sauvignon Blanc Rapel Valley, 8 % Semillion from old vines in Apalta, 40,000 cases, $12

CUVEE ALEXANDRE CHARDONNAY 2007

COLOR   Light Maize

AROMA   Chablis-like bouquet, muted sweet fruits; flowers and spices

BODY   Medium, Lots of fruit, Good Complexity, Concentrated

PALATE   Tropical fruits, backed by minerals, layers of Citrus

FINISH   Smooth, mild acidity, Refreshing

OUTSTANDING

85% Aged in oak for 10 months, 11,620 cases, Single vineyard from Casablanca Valley, Atalayas, 100% Chardonnay, $23

CUVEE ALEXANDRE CABERNET SAUVIGNON 2007

COLOR   Intense Violet, Almost Black

AROMA   Big Bouquet of Red Fruits, feel the oak, herbs abound

BODY   Medium to Full, Subtle, Round Tannins, Well Structured

PALATE   Smooth, Layers of Fruit, Interesting

FINISH   Long and Velvety, Smooth

OUTSTANDING TO GREAT

85% Cab, 15% Merlot, 100% Apalta, Aged in French oak Barrels for 10 months, $27

CLOS APALTA 2007

COLOR   Black with Purple hues

AROMA   Wonderful Inviting Bouquet of Black fruit, complex spices

BODY   Full, Complex, Layers of Berries, Tones of Minerals, Spices

PALATE   Velvety Smooth, almost creamy fruit, Elegant, Very Special

FINISH   Silk, Very long and languid, French Style

GREAT

61% Carmenere, 24% Cab, Merlot, Petit Verdot complete; Single Vineyard in Apalta; longer hang time made this vintage very special, 2 years in new French oak, untreated, unfiltered, Great Carmenere makes this wine original, with its own special character, $100

LOMA LARGA VINEYARDS

Located in the unique Casablanca Valley, Loma Larga, which means "wide sloping mountain side" is a boutique vineyard making delicious and individualistic wines. Led by its young CEO, Luis Felipe Diaz, originally an engineer, and his talented and creative French winemaker Emeric Geneviere-Montignac, Loma Larga has exploited the sunny, yet foggy mountain valley, with cold winds blowing in from the almost freezing Pacific Ocean, in a most original manner.

Having studied the make up of the soil on their precious plantation for over 10 years, Loma Larga has planted sauvignon blanc and chardonnay grapes in the lower valley, which all of the Casablanca vineyards have done; but they planted cabernet franc and malbec on the sunny hillsides, along with syrah. The results, which have been developed over various harvests, exploit the special terroir found therein.

With only 2 years of bottling, they have some killer, unique wines that exceed all expectations, offering a very French structure to the special Chilean grapes found at Loma Larga. In 2008, Loma Larga produced only 9000 cases in total This amount will increase in the near future. There is no pretense to this company: they make wonderful wines, simply packaged, that let the minerality and fruity flavors come through in products that clearly improve in the bottle, and can handle 5 years or more of development to reach their peak performance. Prior to my trip to Chile, I had never heard of this vineyard; now I am a believer that they will make important wines for many years to come. www.lomalarga.com; info@lomalarga.com

LOMA LARGA SAUVIGNON BLANC 2008

COLOR   Maize
AROMA   Smooth, inviting, soft citrus bouquet, mineral tonalities
BODY   Medium, well balanced, delicious
PALATE   Round, smooth, almost sancerre-like
FINISH   Extremely smooth with a long ending; superb

GREAT
Aged in 100% stainless steel, 600 cases, hand selected, extremely low yield, very special, perhaps best sauvignon blanc from Chile, $15

LOMA LARGA CHARDONNAY 2008

COLOR   Deep Yellow
AROMA   Fresh, inviting; Tropical bouquet: fruit/
              minerals
BODY   Medium, very refreshing, terrific fruit/mineral
              complexity
PALATE   Smooth, very tropical version of Chablis, well
              balanced
FINISH   Smooth citrus finish,

OUTSTANDING TO GREAT

2007 Even better, improves over 3 years, aged in oak, 620 cases, very low yield, very French and very special $15

LOMA LARGA PINOT NOIR 2007

COLOR   Violet
AROMA   Full and inviting; Round bouquet of berries
BODY   Full, Older years even better, Delicious
PALATE   Very smooth, earthy, very special Burgundian
              Roundness
FINISH   Smooth, wonderful, long and full

GREAT

900 cases, super low yield, 1% Chard; 100% aged in oak, with 15% new, for 10 months; no fining, no filtering, low sulfate, very natural, special terroir. As with most of the production, the style is very French, the fruits very tropical; superb at $25

LOMA LARGA, MERLOT, 2007

COLOR   Deep Purple
AROMA   Great bouquet of fruits, promises a lot
BODY   Full, round, Berries/spices/mildly peppery,
              complex
PALATE   Very smooth, Full, complex berry taste,
              Earthy, Delicious
FINISH   Smooth and long, Terrific

GREAT

This is a WOW wine, with complexity, 5% Malbec, a special wine, very sensual; no oak! Less than 600 cases; $15 keep it and age it.

LOMA LARGA MALBEC 2007

COLOR   Intense Fuschia
AROMA   Extremely inviting, mixed fruits and spices
BODY   Very full and rewarding, structured, smooth
PALATE   Silky smooth, complex, delicious
FINISH   Elegant, smooth, long and languid

GREAT
A rare Chilean Malbec, oak is very subtle, 5% Syrah, and all grapes from Casablanca mountainside; 1 year in French oak; will and should age for peak performance; original; First vintage, $18

LOMA LARGA CABERNET FRANC 2007

COLOR   Very Deep Purple
AROMA   Smoky tannins, inviting, Full, Round bouquet
    of Fruits
BODY   Variety of Dark Fruit, Smooth, Easy
PALATE   Dominated by variety of Fruits, Full, Round
FINISH   Smooth, long, delicious

OUTSTANDING
Needs to age 90% Cab Franc, Syrah, Malbec, Merlot finishes, 1100 cases, 100% Casablanca valley, 60% new oak, hand selected, low yield, will age well, $18

LOMA LARGA SYRAH, 2007

COLOR   Deep Purple
AROMA   Inviting bouquet of mixed fruits
BODY   Smooth and sensuous; Fruits/Spices/herbs/
    flowers
PALATE   Fleshy, sensuous, Very smooth, lots of fruits
FINISH   Smooth and marvelous, under-aged Lolita in
    lace

GREAT
900 cases, low yield, French-like, 25% in new oak, rest in used oak, all grapes from Casablanca Valley, $22

LOMA LARGA RAPSODIA 2007

COLOR   Black
AROMA   Berry dominated bouquet, Inviting
BODY   Full, lots of Fruit, Young
PALATE Fruity, Big, will age to be fabulous, but still
        young
FINISH Smooth, long

OUTSTANDING

Needs to age to be great; 70% Syrah, Malbec and Cab Franc complete blend; only 200 cases, extremely low yield, entry in stainless Steel, rolled in oak barrels, everything done by hand; $30

LOS VASCOS

Based in a magnificent 185 year old vineyard, in Colchagua Valley, some 40 kilometers from the Pacific Ocean, and 200 kilometers Southwest of Santiago, Los Vascos is the Chilean base of the Lafite Rothschild family of wines. The vineyard of 580 hectares is one of the largest single vineyards in the country and is ensconced in a 3600 hectare farm. In 1988, Lafitte purchased Los Vascos and greatly upgraded and expanded its facilities. Additionally, a replanting program was put in place and yields were greatly reduced. Up to this time, the previous owners had sold all their product to Concha y Toro for the latter's premium wine production. Although the French management had some rough years adjusting to South America, today Los Vascos is producing magnificent wines worthy of the Rothschild name. Los Vascos Gran Reserve and Los Vascos Le Dix are the leading brands of the Vineyard and are truly great wines on an international scale. Interestingly, the latter two wines are aged in oak barrels fabricated by Lafite Rothschild in France. All other Los Vascos wines are aged in stainless steel with no oak at all. "Los Vascos" means "The Basques", honoring the origins of the founders of the original vineyards.

The winery today is cutting edge technically with state of the art computer controls. 450,000 cases are produced annually. Cabernet Sauvignon vines make up over 90% of the vineyard. The oldest vines are 60 years old, although the majority are divided between plots 12 years old and others 20 to 55 years old. The vineyard is the largest in Colchagua Valley, located at the foot of Mount Canaten.

Los Vascos accepts visitors with previous reservations. A small store and tasting area is open to tourists. www.vinalosvascos.com; losvascos@losvascos.cl

LOS VASCOS SAUVIGNON BLANC 2009

COLOR   Pale Yellow
AROMA   Very Inviting, somewhat complex, Citrus/
        Mineral bouquet
BODY   Round, Subtle, Lots of Fruit and Minerals;
        herbal notes
PALATE Refreshing, Crisp, Complex blend of fruits/
        minerals,
FINISH Smooth, long, delicious

OUTSTANDING TO GREAT
100% Sauvignon Blanc, 85% from Casablanca, 10% Leyda, 5% Colchagua Valley; 25,000 cases, Very interesting wine, $12

LOS VASCOS CHARDONNAY 2009

COLOR   Yellow
AROMA   Alluring bouquet of citrus and minerals
BODY   Round, Complex blend of many fruits,
        Delicious
PALATE Smooth as silk; Ocean overtones, Refreshing,
        Wonderful
FINISH Velvety, long and lusty, like an ocean breeze in
        summer

OUTSTANDING TO GREAT
100% Chardonnay, no oak, 60% Casablanca, 40% Colchagua Valley, 40,000
cases, $12

LOS VASCOS CABERNET SAUVIGNON 2008

COLOR   Intense Violet
AROMA   Very inviting bouquet of red berry, minerals,
        Enticing
BODY   Full, Complex mix of berries, with mineral
        overtones
PALATE Subtle, smooth, Delicious, True Terroir felt
        with no oak
FINISH Velvet! Long and languid; Delicious

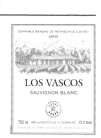

GREAT
100% Cab, no oak, 350,000 cases, Incredible value for only $12

LOS VASCOS GRAN RESERVE 2007

COLOR   Deep Purple
AROMA   Enticing bouquet of red berry, mineral
        overtones; complex, inviting
BODY   Beyond smooth, Very Round, Structured,
        Subtle Spices
PALATE Superb, Complex blend of Cassis, Red Berries, spices, coffee
FINISH Silky smooth, long lasting, Wonderful

GREAT
75% Cab, with Carmenere, Syrah, Cot; 1 year in Lafitte oak Barrels, 40% new;
1 year more in Bottles, 100% Colchagua Valley 45,000 cases NOTE: the
1997 Gran Reserve, which did not have Carmenere, has aged magnificently
and is a real treat; deep purple, wonderful body and long, languid finish; this
wine ages very well! $30. Amazing value

LOS VASCOS LE DIX 2006

COLOR   Deep Purple, almost Black
AROMA   Great Bouquet of Dark Fruits, very
        Bordeaux in Character
BODY   Full, Smooth as Silk, Structured and
        Complex
PALATE Subtle, Elegant, French in style, Round
        fruit, Delicious
FINISH Velvety smooth, languidly long, Wonderful

GREAT

Icon, 84% Cab, 10% Carmenere, rest Syrah; first vintage not 100% Cab; aged 18 months in 100% new Lafitte oak barrels, then 1 year in bottles; totally French in style, but with great tropical fruits makes for an original effort with complexity and elegance; made from 70 year old vines, produced in limited quantities (3,000 to 5,000 cases per annum) depending on each year's quality (2005 did not have a Le Dix), $50

MATETIC

The Matetic family created an ultra-modern winery, with very sleek installations, that produces boutique style wines with vineyards in the San Antonio Valley, just 45 minutes from Santiago. Founded in 1999, foreign consultants were contracted to ensure the biodynamic nature of the plantations. The architecture is beautiful but extremely functional. All of the vineyards are certified organic and are biodynamic. With a wonderful Bread and Breakfast Inn and a chic restaurant, Matetic is extremely tourist friendly and is a very enjoyable location for visitors. www.matetic.com. info@mateticvineyards.com

MATETIC SAUVIGNON BLANC COASTAL EQ 2009

COLOR   Pale Maize
AROMA   Subtle whiffs of citrus fruit
BODY   Refreshing, dense, lovely citrus taste. principally grapefruit
PALATE   Very round and enjoyable
FINISH   Long and smooth

VERY GOOD TO OUTSTANDING
100% Sauvignon Blanc, from Rosario subsector, plantations 8 miles from the Pacific Ocean, EQ represents equilibrium, which is the goal of the winery in planting its organic grapes. $18

MATETIC CHARDONNAY EQ 2009

COLOR   Yellow
AROMA   Bouquet of pears, minerals
BODY   Full, interesting layers of fruits, subtle touches
          of oak
PALATE   Round, good structure, smoky blends of fruits
FINISH   Long and smooth

OUTSTANDING
90% Aged in oak for 9 months, very low yields, 920 cases $22

MATETIC PINOT NOIR EQ 2008

COLOR   VIOLET
AROMA   Enticing bouquet of red berries
BODY   Medium, Very round with good structure
PALATE   Smooth, lots of berries, muted, good density
FINISH   Long, smooth,

OUTSTANDING
100% Pinot Noir, 9 months in French oak, extremely low yield, $28

MATETIC SYRAH EQ 2008

COLOR   Purple
AROMA   Inviting bouquet of dark cherry and minerals
BODY   Full, very French in style, dense, great balance,
          Elegant
PALATE   Firm and Round, well structured, subtle
          mineral tones
FINISH   Smooth, languid and sensual

OUTSTANDING TO GREAT
100% Syrah, 1 year in French oak, $32

MATETIC SYRAH CORALILLO 2008

COLOR   Violet
AROMA   Inviting bouquet of flowers, red fruits
BODY   Dense, Full, complex layers of smoky fruit,
          floral overtones
PALATE   Well structured, Round, Firm, Long
FINISH   Smooth, languid, delicious

OUTSTANDING TO GREAT
100% Syrah, 1 year in French oak, extremely low yield, highly selective, $22

MONTES

The magnificent winery is located at the foothills of the Andes in the section of Apalta, the Chilean equivalent of Bordeaux. Soft classical music serenades the French oak barrels of aging wine, sunlight brightens the ambiance for the workers to better see the grapes for selection, the layout respects the tao of the region; Montes winery is like vinification heaven. Feng Shui principles directed the design and placement of the entire winery and vineyard.

The history of Montes begins and depends on Aurelio Montes, a respected wine consultant. Starting with smarts, guts, and a vision, Montes joined with 3 other partners to build from scratch one of the most respected wineries in the country. Recently passed in sales by Ventisquero, for which Montes is head consultant, Vina Montes is the sixth largest winery in Chile, with 700,000 cases produced, of which 95% are exported.

Aurelio Junior is in charge of the management and is a brilliant winemaker on his own, having worked in many wineries prior to joining his family's business. He is a practicing Catholic who follows zen philosophy in running the winery. Montes' believes that the best Pinot Noir comes from the Leyda sector (very close to the Pacific Ocean). Luis Miguel, a world renowned Mexican singer, asked Aurelio to make him a special Pinot Noir, so he could have a wine to share with his girl friend(s). The solution was a Leyda Pinot Noir!

Another Gem from Aurelio: Oak is like salt on meat; it can bring out the best flavor when properly applied; too much kills the taste! The winery, as so many of the great wineries of Chile, employs a gravitational system to move the grapes in a gentle manner without machines. Montes Alpha Cabernet Sauvignon 1987 was the company's first premium wine and set an example for other wineries to join in making Chile a producer of upscale wines to challenge France and the U.S. among others. In 1996, Montes launched Montes M, their first Icon wine, in a Bordeaux style that ranks among the best produced in South America.

Similarly, Montes claims the first full Carmenere, Purple Angel, (at least 75% of the wine must be Carmenere Grape) released in 2005. Regardless of who is first at anything, Montes is consecrated today as a leader in Premium wines for the country. They are not alone but they are up there with a number of absolute top wines, from Chile, to compete anywhere at any time!

Douglas Murray is the partner responsible for the fabulous marketing of Montes wines. Seemingly overnight, Montes became well-known for its high quality wines, even before, Montes had its own winery. Aurelio and Douglas are the two remaining of the original partners. The symbol of the winery, an angel, comes from the belief that an angel has saved him from near death experiences too many times to be just coincidental. Hence, since the beginning, the owners felt they needed to have an angel watching over them for their venture to succeed. As a result, there are beautiful statues of angels throughout the winery and on all of their labels, especially the icons.

Upon entering the magnificent winery, one feels the very positive force and sensibility that inspired the company to have achieved so much in such a short period of time. Montes is extremely tourist friendly with fabulous vistas on the nearby Andes and a great tasting room in one of the most beautiful wineries one can see. Montes offers some fabulous tours always ending in a great tasting. Reservations essential. lafinca@monteswines.com; www.monteswines.com

MONTES SAUVIGNON BLANC LIMITED SELECTION 2009

COLOR	Pale Yellow
AROMA	Intense bouquet of citrus
BODY	Round, Full, Elegant, Very special
PALATE	Lovely in the mouth, Complex, ultra-smooth, mineral overtones
FINISH	Long, smooth, mild citrus

OUTSTANDING TO GREAT
100% Leyda Valley, 30,000 cases, 8 Hectares near Pacific Ocean, all stainless steel, $15

MONTES ALPHA CHARDONNAY

COLOR	Maize
AROMA	Enticing bouquet of tropical fruits, minerals abound
BODY	Round, Creamy taste of citrus, banana, minerals
PALATE	Exceedingly smooth, muted citrus, minerals
FINISH	Long, delicious, silky, Opulent

OUSTANDING TO GREAT
100% Casablanca Valley, 1 year in oak, 22,000 cases, low yield, recalls Chablis at its best, $18

MONTES ALPHA PINOT NOIR D.O. LEYDA 2007

COLOR	Purple
AROMA	Inviting, minerals surround the black berry bouquet
BODY	Medium, Round, soft tannins, Very Smooth, Expressive

PALATE   Elegant, Silky, fabulous taste of muted berries; well balanced.
FINISH   Very long and languid, Velvety Smooth

GREAT
100% Leyda Valley, extremely low yield, 2nd Harvest, 40% in new French oak, 30% unoaked, 3000 cases; a very special wine $20

MONTES ALPHA CABERNET SAUVIGNON 2007

COLOR   Intense Violet
AROMA   Very inviting, Rich Bouquet of dark berries
BODY   Full, Round, Great fruit/mineral blend, Burgundian
PALATE   Elegant, Silky Smooth, creamy in texture, Complex layers of fruit
FINISH   Languidly smooth, delicious, Sensual, silky

GREAT
90% Cab, 10% Merlot, 100% Apalta, aged 100% in French oak, followed by 1 year in bottles, Incredible quality of delicious wine, $20

MONTES ALPHA SYRAH 2007

COLOR   Intense Fuchsia
AROMA   Alluring, round bouquet of berries and smoky spices
BODY   Medium, soft, Easy
PALATE   Round, Smooth
FINISH   Smooth, very nice

OUTSTANDING
 90% Syrah, 7% Cab, 3% Viognier, 100% Apalta, very low yield, $20

MONTES ALPHA CARMENERE 2007

COLOR   Deep Purple
AROMA   Intense, Inviting bouquet of Dark Berries, mild oak; mineral whiffs
BODY   Full, Complex, Top-notch Depth, Well-structured
PALATE   Big and Strong, lots of spices modify the berries
FINISH   Smooth, but very individualistic

OUTSTANDING
90% Carmenere,10% Cab, 4000 cases, sells out early each vintage, 100% Marchigue,(in Mapuche, means land of wind and witches), a desert stretch of land near coastal mountains; $20

MONTES M 2006

COLOR   Deep Purple
AROMA   Enticing, delicate bouquet of Fruits, Burgundian
        to the nose
BODY   Full, Velvety, Breathtakingly smooth and
        delicious
PALATE Soft Tannins, concentrated, Complex layers of
        dark fruit
FINISH Smooth, silky smooth, 45 minutes to fully open;
        very rewarding

GREAT

80% Cab, 10% Cab Franc, 5% each Petit Verdot/Merlot; Apalta, 18 months
in French oak; 3000 cases, extremely low yield of 5 Tons per Hectare, Original
Icon (one of a number now), sets the bar for top Chilean wines, $80

MONTES FOLLY 2006

COLOR   Black
AROMA   Intriguing bouquet of mixed berries
        muted by oak, many spices and herbs
BODY   Full, Round, very well structured, layers
        of complex fruit
PALATE Robust, Great Depth of various dark berries, minerals and spices
FINISH Dense and smooth, long and lingering; terrific

GREAT

100% Syrah, from the mountainsides of Apalta, far up at a 45 degree angle,
very special grapes, literally handpicked, aged for 18 months in new French
oak; Aurelio considers this is folly or crazy idea to plant so far up the
mountainside, especially the Syrah grape, fantastic label painted by Ralph
Steadman, a true collector's item and 2nd icon of group, 2000 cases, $90

MONTES PURPLE ANGEL 2006

COLOR   Black!
AROMA   Phenomenal bouquet of dark berries,
        minerals, spices, Enticing!
BODY   Full and Complex, Layers of Berries, Sensual,
        Enthralling
PALATE Velvety Smooth, Dense and Structured, Perfection!
FINISH Long, voluptuous, from bouquet to sensual last drop, Black lace!

GREAT

92% Carmenere, half Apalta, half Marchigue, 8% Petit Verdot, 18 months in new French oak, For this writer the best Montes icon, and a sexy, top notch Carmenere, a work of genius at half the price of the others, $50.

MONTES LATE HARVEST GERWURZTRAMINER 2008

COLOR   Deep Maize
AROMA   Sweet, whiffs of Fruit, Very enticing
BODY   Liquid Jam, very Full, subtly sweet, not sugary
PALATE   Smooth, creamy, well balanced, dense
FINISH   Sweet, smooth, Clean, terrific ending to a meal

OUTSTANDING

Curico Valley, 50% Riesling but it is the Gerwurztraminer that sets the pace, $25

MONTGRAS

Situated on one of the oldest vineyards in Chile, Montgras is a modern, $20 million, state of the art winery in the heart of Colchagua Valley. Founded in 1992 by the Gras Brothers, MontGras, now has a total of 2000 hectares and exports 650,000 cases annually. Montgras' production is 97% from its own vineyards.

The Merlot vineyards were discovered to have large sections of Carmenere and MontGras has maintained those plantations to make some wonderful Carmenere and Carmenere blends.

The unusually talented chief Winemaker, Santiago Margozzini, has raised the level of Montgras signature wines to among the best in Chile. Until 2008, Paul Hobbs advised on the icon wines.

The vineyard is very tourist friendly, with previous reservations, and has great tasting areas, as well as a neat little store. Tours include blind tastings, picking your own grapes, experiencing pairing wines with food, and even making your own wine! There are horseback tours, as the winery has its own horses, and great trails up the Ninquen mountainside for even better views. www.montgras.cl; TOURS@montgras.cl; www.mgproperties.cl; www.ninquen.cl; www.intrigua.cl

MONTGRAS SAUVIGNON BLANC AMARAL 2009

COLOR   Light clear Yellow
AROMA   Flowers and spices compliment a Citrus
        Bouquet; notes of the sea
BODY   Elegant, soft, almost spiritual; waifs of citrus
        and minerals
PALATE Soft and round, lemony, but smooth, like
        tasting a breeze
FINISH Smooth and very refreshing

OUTSTANDING

Amaral means to love the sea, 100% Sauvignon Blanc, 3000 cases, low yield, from Leyda vineyards 26 miles from Pacific Ocean, marine terroir is clear in the taste, alleuvial deposits of stone, granite. $16

MONTGRAS CHARDONNAY AMARAL 2009

COLOR   Yellow
AROMA   Alluring bouquet of fruits and minerals
BODY   Full, complex tastes of fruit and granite;
         Structured
PALATE   Smooth, vague sucrosity, terrific flavors of
         fruits, Elegant
FINISH   Smooth, refreshingly elegant

OUTSTANDING TO GREAT
Uncommonly complex, very reduced production (180 cases) with hand picked
selected grapes, 70% in new French oak, $20

MONTGRAS MERLOT RESERVA 2008

COLOR   Intense Violet
AROMA   Enticing bouquet of dark fruits and minerals,
         with a touch of spice
BODY   Medium, smooth, blackberries, granite, spice
         from carmenere
PALATE   Round, structured, oak overtones,
FINISH   Smooth, lots of fruit to the end

OUTSTANDING
90% Merlot, 10% Carmenere, the latter giving some complexity and spiciness;
good combination, Colchagua Valley, 8 months in oak, 50,000 cases, $12

MONTGRAS CARMENERE RESERVA 2008

COLOR   Deep Purple
AROMA   Wonderful bouquet of dark berries and spices
BODY   Big berry taste, Round, full,
PALATE   Distinctive taste, old vine carmenere, lots of
         spices with red berry
FINISH   Terrific long lasting ending makes you want more

GREAT
10% Cab, 30,000 cases, 5 months in oak, 50% new, hand-picked, 100%
Colchagua Valley, must buy at $12

MONTGRAS CABERNET SAUVIGNON RESERVA 2008

COLOR   Deep Purple

AROMA   Inviting full bodied bouquet of black cherry
and currants

BODY   Full, lots of Fruit, very smooth, uncommon
depth

PALATE   Round, elegant fruits, like a punch in a velvet glove

FINISH   Smooth, long, delicious

OUTSTANDING TO GREAT

60,000 Cases, biggest seller of winery, 15% from Maipo, 85% from Colchagua
Valley, 100% Cab, 8 months in 100% new oak, $12

MONTGRAS QUATRO 2008

COLOR   Almost black Intense Violet

AROMA   Complex bouquet of many dark grapes,
inviting and original

BODY   Full, Intense, balanced mix of currants and
dark grapes

PALATE   Interesting and intriguing mix of berries,
overtones of spices

FINISH   Smooth. Lingering,

OUTSTANDING

Blend of 4 grapes all grown by Montgras: Cab, almost half, Carmenere,
Malbec, Syrah. 100% aged in new and used oak for 11 months, 20,000 cases,
drink now, $17

ANTU NINQUEN SYRAH 2007

COLOR   Deep Purple

AROMA   Inviting bouquet of Mixed berries and minerals

BODY   Full, very smooth, oak rounds off the taste

PALATE   Round, structured and very smooth

FINISH   Smooth, languishing and delicious

OUTSTANDING TO GREAT

100% Syrah, long skin contact, aged in oak, 50% new, Paul Hobbs helped
develop this wine, $19

ANTU NINQUEN 2007

COLOR   Deep Purple
AROMA   Strong bouquet of blackberries and wild spices
BODY   Full, Round, very smooth and complex
PALATE   Well structured, Smooth and Strong, French
         style, very sensual
FINISH   Smooth, long lasting, just terrific

GREAT

70% Cab, 30% Carmenere, 22 months in oak barrels, 50% new; the best wine of the group, though not the most expensive, Blind taste it against any full bodied California wine, a Paul Hobbs development til 2008, $20

NINQUEN 2006

COLOR   Deep Purple
AROMA   Alluring notes of blackberries, firm bouquet
BODY   Full, lots of fruit, Well balanced
PALATE   Round and very smooth, good concentration
         and well structured
FINISH   Smooth, very long, easy ending

GREAT

65% Cab, 35% Carmenere, 21 months in barrels, predominantly French and new, wonderful blend, Montgras exploits its terrific Carmenere to perfection, Flagship wine, another terrific effort with help from Paul Hobbs, $40

INTRIGA CABERNET SAUVIGNON 2006

COLOR   Very Deep Purple
AROMA   Enticing bouquet, Bordeaux in style
BODY   Full, Very interesting, very French
PALATE   Round, Firm, Well balanced,
FINISH   Smooth, Velvety, Delicious

GREAT

100% Cab, 100% Maipo Valley, aged 17 months in 85% in new French oak, 4,400 cases, $38

PEREZ CRUZ

The vineyards are located in the Maipo Valley, some 30 miles south of Santiago, surrounded by the foothills of the Andes Mountains. Characterized by thermal oscillation of 25 degrees Farenheit, between night and day, the climate offers a gradual ripening of the grapes, time for full tannin development and a long hang time for increased fruit concentration.

Perez Cruz has 150 hectares of vineyards, of which 70% is Cabernet, 10% is Carmenere and 5% each of Syrah, Petit Verdot, Malbec and Merlot. All the wine production comes from their own estate vineyards. The wines are made with very low yield, hand picked grapes. The wines are bottled around 1 year and a half after harvest and remain around 5 months in bottles prior to shipping. 62,000 cases are produced annually.

The winery is very modern, both in its outlook and its architecture. The building housing the winery is very modern, constructed out of laminated wood, with a low stone wall base, housing some 65,000 square feet. With a very efficient, gravity induced, modern wine processing system, Perez Cruz turns out top quality wines. In general, the reds I tasted were excellent but needed more aging. I have a fondness for Perez Cruz as it was one of the first Carmeneres I "discovered" when opening my Brazilian restaurant.

Perez Cruz is definitely tourist friendly and modern architecture is a delight for visitors to view. Tours are daily, Monday to Friday, with previous reservations. Tours vary in cost and in length, depending on how many wines are to be consumed. mjconcha@perezcruz.com; www.perezcruz.com

PEREZ CRUZ CABERNET SAUVIGNON RESERVA 2008

COLOR   Deep Purple
AROMA   Inviting fruits/berries make a terrific bouquet, flowery
BODY   Medium to Full, Big on Fruit, Round, needs time to open
PALATE   Round, touches of herbs, clearly young but terrific
FINISH   Smooth, long, excellent

OUTSTANDING
90% Cab, remainder being Syrah, Merlot, Cot. Over 50,000 cases, 12 months in oak, 65% American oak, 35% French oak, no fining, As good as it is, it will be better with age. 2007 was a great year, maybe best ever for Chile. Still early for 2008. $15

PEREZ CRUZ CARMENERE RESERVA LIMITED EDITION 2008

COLOR   Deep Violet
AROMA   Fruity, spice overtones, minerality; 2003 had
        great bouquet
BODY   Very fruity and big. 2003 very round, full,
        strong, smooth.
PALATE Young but outstanding; 2003: Mineral notes,
        Black fruit
FINISH Smooth, long; 2003 fabulous, like velvet

OUTSTANDING
Though very young; more aged versions are superb; 92% Carmenere, 8%
Syrah; 3500 cases, increasing to 4000 in future vinages. The 2003 was
significantly smoother, more structured and developed than the young 2008.
I tasted the 2008 only a short time after bottling, so age is definitely a factor;
Again, 2007 is superb. $20

PEREZ CRUZ COT 2008

COLOR   Deep Violet
AROMA   Inviting, sensual in bouquet
BODY   Medium, spicy/floral notes complement dark
        berries
PALATE Round, structured, young
FINISH Smooth, long, clean

VERY GOOD
90% Cot (French version of Malbec, not as big as Argentine version), rest
Carmenere and Petit Verdot; 14 months in oak barrels, $20

PEREZ CRUZ SYRAH RESERVA LIMITED EDITION 2007

COLOR   Clear Violet
AROMA   Smoky dark berry bouquet with pepper notes
BODY   Medium, ripened berries, ideal for pork loin
        dishes
PALATE Light, smooth, easy, Round
FINISH Easy and smooth

VERY GOOD
90% Syrah, 10% Carmenere, latter gives structure and body to a light wine; 8
months bottle aged after oak aging; low yields, 2000 cases, $25

PEREZ CRUZ LIGUAI 2006

COLOR   Intense Violet
AROMA   Smooth, inviting, subtle
BODY   Full, dark fruits, muted notes of wood/ peppers Very Smooth
PALATE   Round, delicious, complex, layered and structured
FINISH   Smooth, long and languid; very sensual

OUTSTANDING TO GREAT

40% Each of Syrah and Carmenere, 20% Cabernet Sauvignon; Very low yield, 1200 cases, 16 months in oak, Liguai means "guess what" in Mapuche, $40

PEREZ CRUZ QUELEN 2006

COLOR   Deep, Dark Purple
AROMA   Mild, elegant bouquet of red berries and minerals
BODY   Full, very big red fruits, Round, Smooth, Structured
PALATE   Very layered, complex, concentrated, overtones of minereals
FINISH   Smooth, round and long lasting; very enjoyable

OUTSTANDING TO GREAT

Petit Verdot, Carmenere, and Cot blend; 100% in French oak barrels for 14 months, Icon, well aged and delicious; $50

SANTA RITA

Santa Rita is the third largest winery in Chile. A magnificent winery that includes an upscale hotel, the Casa Real, Santa Rita is set in a fabulous 100 acre estate and has a very interesting restaurant, Dona Paula, a museum (Museo Andino) of the founder's collection of Pre-Columbian art, and a terrific tasting room and store. A stop at the Santa Rita winery is essential for anyone desiring to learn more about wine and the country of Chile. Sleeping over at Casa Real is icing on the cake.

Santa Rita founded in 1880, was one of the first companies to use imported vines from Europe. Primarily known as a wine producer for the domestic market, it was acquired by the late Ricardo Claro in 1980 and has developed a fabulous line of premium wines. It's vineyards are located in the premium regions of Chile: Maipo, Colchagua, Casablanca, Curico, Leyda, Limari and Apalta. Andres Ilabaca makes the fabulous new premium wines and is a knowledgeable and very informative guide to the details of Chilean winemaking and their regions. Hector Torres, the export manager is talented and experienced in dealing with interested visitors to Santa Rita.

Santa Rita's introductory line of Santa Rita 120 maintains an excellent varietal selection in the $8 range. Additionally, the Reservas at $12 and the Medalla Real at $18 are all excellent wines. There are 3 icon wines written about below, with the Casa Real being the traditional flagship wine.

Santa Rita is very tourist friendly with a fabulous hotel, Casa Real, which was formerly the manor house for the estate. Additionally, La Casa de Dona Paula Restaurant is a national monument and serves wonderful Chilean food, as well as many international dishes for lunch. There is a museum, Andino Museum, next to the hotel that houses an impressive collection of pre- Columbian artifacts. www.santarita.com; ilanderos@santarita.cl

SANTA RITA SAUVIGNON BLANC 2009

COLOR   Clear Lemon
AROMA   Firm Fruity bouquet, grapefruit; very inviting
BODY   Healthy and smooth, delicious grapefruit
        notes
PALATE Lovely, enjoyable, no acidity; have very cold
        with fish
FINISH Long and smooth, round and dry; very enjoyable

OUTSTANDING
Very special, no after taste nor strong acidity, 7000 cases, D.O. from Casablanca Valley, $10

SANTA RITA SAUVIGNON BLANC MEDALLA REAL 2008

COLOR	Pale Maize, inviting lively color
AROMA	Wonderfully enticing and complex; layers of fruits/minerals
BODY	Round, delicious; many contrasts of sweet and citrus fruits
PALATE	Complex, Shades of Chablis w/ Tropical Fruits; Sensual
FINISH	Smooth, long, delicious

OUTSTANDING TO GREAT

Low yield, Leyda Valley, no oak, very special wine, the best of French style with tropical grapes; $18

SANTA RITA CHARDONNAY MEDALLA REAL 2008

COLOR	Deep Yellow almost Gold
AROMA	Complex, citrus and pear, Extremely inviting
BODY	Very smooth, lots of fruit, mixed tonalities, delicious
PALATE	Complex, different notes of fruit, minerals; wonderful taste
FINISH	Smooth, long, very round and rewarding

OUTSTANDING TO GREAT

8 Months in oak, very low yield, from Limari vineyard 400 kilometers north of Santiago, only second vintage, very special wine, $18

SANTA RITA CARMENERE RESERVA 2008

COLOR	Deep Purple
AROMA	Smoky, Spicy, Very Round Bouquet of Dark Berry
BODY	Big, Strong, Full, Lots of Fruit and Spices
PALATE	Terrific, complex, lots of mineral overtones, Spice, Berry
FINISH	Smooth, long, languid. Special

OUTSTANDING

8 Months in oak, 20,000 cases, 50% sold to U.S., 100% Carmenere from Colchagua Valley, $12

SANTA RITA CABERNET SAUVIGNON RESERVA 2007

COLOR   Crimson
AROMA   Light, fruity bouquet
BODY   Very smooth, nice mineral taste
           complimenting red fruits
PALATE   Round, medium firmness, straightforward,
           soft tannins
FINISH   Smooth, very easy, soft

VERY GOOD
100,000 Cases, 10 months in oak, 100% Maipo valley, Santa Rita's best seller
in U. S., $12

SANTA RITA CARMENERE MEDALLA REAL 2008

COLOR   Deep Purple, almost Black
AROMA   Strong, Inviting, Black Berry, w/ Minerality,
           Spices
BODY   Very Full, Lots of Mature Fruit, Mineral
           Overtones
PALATE   Very smooth, Full, Complex, Strong and
           Masculine
FINISH   Smooth, Fantastic, Bordeaux style but tropical, long

GREAT
100% Carmenere from Colchaga Valley, 15% Apalta, 85% Marchigue (Close
to Ocean), 70% new French oak, rest used, for 10 months, Superb, $18

SANTA RITA CABERNET SAUVIGNON GRAN RESERVA 2007

COLOR   Deep Purple
AROMA   Strong, Very Inviting, Black Currents and
           Minerals Bouquet
BODY   Smooth but Very Full, terrific mix of fruit and
           minerals
PALATE   Round, should age very well, but excellent
           right now
FINISH   Smooth, long lasting Great Compliment to Steak, Lobster

GREAT
9% Cab Franc, rest Cab Sauvignon; 14 months in French oak, 40% new, Low
yield, 100% Maipo Valley, Fabulous wine for $60

SANTA RITA TRIPLE C 2005

COLOR   Intense Violet Hues
AROMA   Big, round inviting bouquet, complex mineral touches
BODY   Full, dark fruits dominate, minerals and tasty spices
PALATE Round, complex blend of minerals and spices, Terrific
FINISH Smooth, lovely, long, but very masculine,

GREAT

Icon of winery, Maipo Valley, D.O., 55% Cab Franc, 35% Cab
Sauv, 15% Carmenere, Blend varies every year with winemaker's
touch; Each varietal is aged separately for 6 months in new French
oak barrels, then blended and aged another 11 months in new French oak,
giving it an extra complexity and originality, at least 1 year in bottle prior to
shipping; superb, $60

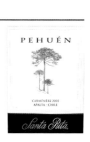

PEHUEN CARMENERE 2005

COLOR   Very Deep Purple
AROMA   Complex, inviting, muted, alluring spices
BODY   Very Smooth, Complex, Deep Dark Berry,
        Mineral/Spice blend
PALATE Round, Full, Structured, Very smooth,
        Concentrated
FINISH Velvety smooth, keeps pleasing. Sensual

GREAT

95% Carmenere, from Apalta, 5% Cab, 20 months in first use oak, bottled for
12 months prior to release, vines date from 1940's, $65

SANTA RITA CASA REAL 2005

COLOR   Black with purple hues
AROMA   Alluringly soft bouquet of black fruits,
        muted by French oak
BODY   Bordeaux in Style, Smooth, Complex,
        Tropical in nature
PALATE Round, Full, Silky, Sensual, Rich in Tannins, Structured
FINISH Long, delicious, languid, Sleek, almost erotic it is so good

GREAT

100% Cabernet, 40 year old vines, super selective harvest, 14 months in new
French oak barrels, followed by 1 year fermentation in bottles, 1500 cases,
some years filtered, some not; not made every year, Flagship of Santa Rita,
$75 FINAL NOTE: I had the pleasure of tasting the 1999 Casa Real, which
was elegant, full bodied and fantastic; this wine definitely grows with age,
Magnificent!

UNDURRAGA

One of the oldest wineries in Chile, some vineyards date back to 1885, the winery was founded by Don Francisco Undurraga, who personally brought over French vines in the 19th century. The vineyards were in the same family until the 21st century. Originally assisted by the Pressac family from Bordeaux, Undurraga is one of the traditional names in winemaking in Chile and still sells 25% of their large production domestically.

The state of the art winery, inaugurated in 2009, is magnificent, if not breathtaking. A traditional location for society weddings, with horse drawn carriages and all of that, Undurraga was purchased, and new management installed, in 2006. New winemakers led by Hernan Amenabar and Alvaro Espinoza (consultant) and an additional 854 newly acquired hectares of vineyards, are giving new life to the company. Some $35 million in new investments, with emphasis on premium wines and a rejuvenation of some old labels, that had been icons in the past, characterize the new approach.

Undurraga sold 1,213,543 cases in 2008, 75% in exports to 67 countries. 10% of production is in sparkling wines.

Undurraga is extremely socially conscious, with part of the sales of their Aliwen wines going to the Mapuche ethnic group, the original Indian occupants of what is now Chile. There remain many vestiges of Indian culture around the winery.

Very tourist friendly, the winery is located a stone's throw from Santiago, and should not be missed. One interesting part of the facilities are the 100 year old adobe wine cellars. With an excellent store and wine tasting facility, the tour of the new winery installations is educational and fun.

During my visit I was struck by the high and innovative quality of the white wines. Rafael Urrejola is the young winemaker in charge of these recent developments and I believe he is one of the new revelatory talents in the industry. I also had the pleasure of meeting Cristobal Duke, the Commercial Director for International Markets. Undurraga has a young, forward thinking team, a beautiful location and a traditional name. It should be very successful in their recent expansion and development. www.undurraga.cl; info@undurrraga.cl

UNDURRAGA TH SAUVIGNON BLANC 2008

COLOR   Pale Yellow
AROMA   Exuberant bouquet of tropical fruits
BODY   Smooth, consistent and juicy
PALATE   Elegant, round and firm, mix of citrus and sweet fruits
FINISH   Smooth, delicious, very crisp and refreshing

OUTSTANDING
100% Sauvignon blanc, 1400 cases, single vineyard, Undurraga makes 3 versions, 1 each from Casablanca Valley, Leyda and Lo Abarca(The best of the group); each are OUTSTANDING, with terrific terroir individuality; TH stands for Terroir Hunter; $20.

UNDURRAGA PINOT NOIR TH 2008

COLOR	Crimson
AROMA	Alluring nose of red berries, woody tones
BODY	Medium, Interesting Complexity of Rasberry/cherry fruit
PALATE	Round, medium structure, easy, Very Smooth
FINISH	Soft, Easy, Smooth

OUTSTANDING
1st Vintage, Casablanca Valley, hand selected, single vineyard, 12 miles from Pacific Ocean; from vines planted in 1998, 10 months in oak, 750 cases, $25

UNDURRAGA ALTAZOR 2006

COLOR	Very Intense Purple
AROMA	Subtle bouquet of Fruits and minerals
BODY	Medium to Full, Smooth and Round, Expressive Individuality
PALATE	Elegant, Complex, Excellent Mineral notes, Delicious
FINISH	Smooth, Long, Great Fruity Ending

OUTSTANDING
Created by Alvaro Espinoza, Chile's premier wine consultant, 55% Cab, supported by Carmenere, Syrah and Merlot; a true icon, low yield, aged 14 months in new oak separately, then 5 months blended, bottle aged for 1 year; $60

UNDURRAGA BRUT SUPREME 2008

COLOR	Gold
AROMA	Bubbly citrus, Champagne feel
BODY	Round, enjoyable
PALATE	Smooth, Champenoise taste,
FINISH	Easy, Very enjoyable

OUTSTANDING
55% Chardonnay, 45% Pinor Noir, very nice Champagne-like wine;
Undurraga traditionally produces various Champagne-like wines, much of
which is sold domestically, large production, Maipo Valley; very interesting,
$30

VENTISQUERO

The winery began production at its brand new, state of the art building in 1998. Located in the heart of the Coastal Maipo Valley, Ventisquero quickly added vineyards in Casablanca and Colchagua Valleys.

Led by chief oenologist, Felipe Tosso, Ventisquero has a young and talented team that is producing quality wines. The ultra-modern architecture houses a gravity fed production center with eco-friendly systems to preserve the natural habitat of the valley, while producing crisp, premium wines, 85% of which are destined for export.

Owned by one of the largest food companies in Chile, AgroSuper, Ventisquero has spared no expense to quickly become the 5th largest producer/exporter of wines in Chile. The name, Ventisquero, derives from a wind, or whirlwind, producing mountain area. Aurelio Montes is the consultant since the winery's inception. www.ventisquero.com

VENTISQUERO SAUVIGNON BLANC QUEULAT GRAN RESERVA 2009

COLOR	Very Pale Yellow
AROMA	Inviting citrus, flowery bouquet, complex, intriguing
BODY	Complex, tropical touches of citrus, flowers and minerals
PALATE	True variety of excellent tastes—fruit, minerals; original
FINISH	Smooth, long and delicious

OUTSTANDING TO GREAT
100% Casablanca valley, no oak, filled with ocean breeze, a wonderfully complex effort; $18

VENTISQUERO CHARDONNAY QUEULAT 2008

COLOR	Maize
AROMA	Minerals dominate an enticing bouquet, with oak muted fruits
BODY	Full, Round, pleasing complexity of minerals and fruit
PALATE	Very special, French style; tropical fruits, balanced, delicious
FINISH	Smooth, juicy and long lasting

OUTSTANDING TO GREAT
8 Months in French oak, 100% Casablanca grapes, Terrific and original, $18

VENTISQUERO GREY CHARDONNAY 2008

COLOR   Maize
AROMA   Chablis-like bouquet of Fruits, minerals
BODY   Complex, smooth, very special
PALATE   Round, Structured, Great fruit blend
FINISH   Slow, languid, smooth, Superb

GREAT
100% Casablanca Valley, 1st Vintage, Grey is name of the magnificent Grey Glacier in Southern Chile; very low yield, specially hand selected grapes; 12 months in French oak, 1000 cases, $29

VENTISQUERO PINOT NOIR GRAN RESERVA 2008

COLOR   Crimson
AROMA   Very inviting; smoky fruit overtones; subtle
BODY   Perfect blend of minerals, fruits, flowers, Great
PALATE   Round, Smooth, surprisingly complex blend of fruits
FINISH   Lovely, smooth, interesting, long

GREAT
100% Casablanca Valley, Long soaks, some aging in French oak, Alejandro Galaz winemaker for the Pinot and the top whites above; low yield, $18

VENTISQUERO GREY MERLOT, 2007

COLOR   Deep Violet
AROMA   Alluring bouquet of smoky fruit
BODY   Full, complex, original, surprisingly complex
PALATE   Smooth, subtle, smoky fruits, complex and provocative
FINISH   Smooth, long, delicious

OUTSTANDING TO GREAT
90% Merlot, 7% Cab, some Syrah; Apalta, 1000 cases in this first vintage, should increase when it goes to world market, $29

VENTISQUERO GREY SYRAH 2007

COLOR   Intense Crimson
AROMA   Very alluring, subtle notes of cedar flavored
        fruits
BODY   Medium to Full, Very Round, Complex for a
        Syrah
PALATE Diverse tastes of Smoky Berries, minerals, Soft
        Structure
FINISH Silky Smooth, languid, special

OUTSTANDING TO GREAT
100% Apalta vines, $29

VENTISQUERO GREY CARMENERE 2007

COLOR   Intense Violet
AROMA   Expressive bouquet of dark berries and spices
BODY   Full, original, lots of spices compliment big dark
        fruits
PALATE Complex, great structure, rewarding tannins,
        Earthy tones
FINISH Smooth, subtle, long lasting

GREAT
90% Carmenere, 8% Cab, 2% Syrah, Maipo, wonderful, soft
Carmenere, represents best of Chile, only $29

VENTISQUERO GREY CABERNET SAUVIGNON 2007

COLOR   Deep Purple
AROMA   Swirls of fruit, bouquet of herbs, spices,
        raspberry
BODY   Round, Full, Complex, Well Structured, Elegant
PALATE Subtle, Smooth, Great mix of fruits, herbs,
        spices
FINISH Smooth like silk, long, wonderful

OUTSTANDING TO GREAT
92% Cab, 8% Carmenere, Maipo Valley, Trinidad vineyard,
$29

VENTISQUERO VERTICE 2006

COLOR   Intense Purple
AROMA   Enticing Bouquet of berries, overtones of cedar
BODY   Full, Elegant, Complex, Well Structured, Special
PALATE Complex, delicious, Very smooth, Bordeaux-like
FINISH Strong, Silky smooth, long lasting

GREAT
second Vintage, Name originates from vertex of two
plantations that compose the wine; Rivals great Bordeaux,
blend of Carmenere and Syrah, Apalta vines, 1400 feet
altitude, John Duval former head of Penfolds is consultant,
one of the top wines from Chile, only $45.

VENTISQUERO PANGEA 2006

COLOR   Intense Purple
AROMA   Subtle, inviting bouquet of deep dark berries
BODY   Round, Elegant, Berries, tones of complex
        minerals
PALATE Elegant, Well Structured, Delicious
FINISH Smooth, long lasting, very special,

GREAT
100% Syrah from Apalta, Red Clay Soils, Pangea is from Greek, meaning the
Mountainous Super-Continent that existed 250 million years ago before the
component continents separated into their current configuration; A union of
2 worlds, as there are 2 winemakers, John Duval from Australia, and Felipe
Tosso from Chile. Icon wine. $60

VERAMONTE

One of the more interesting wineries in Chile, Veramonte is part of a wine group that includes Flowers (Sonoma) and Quintessa (Napa). Agustin Huneeus, the Chilean owner of this group, has used some of California's best consultants to establish this tourist-friendly winery in the valley of Casablanca, a little over an hour from Santiago and some 20 minutes from the Pacific Ocean.

Tour buses come constantly, both from big cruise liners and from the capital. Formerly President of Concha y Toro, Mr. Huneeus located these vineyards as far back as 1990. His vision has created one of Chile's largest contiguous vineyards, with over 1100 planted acres.

The property is surrounded by 10,000 acres of natural desert-like greenbelt, a habitat of animals and plants, and a large lagoon, home to many species of migrating birds.

Veramonte uses sustainable and organic farming practices, attempting to gain maximum flavor and quality from its plantations. The coastal mountains help form a true valley with the nearby Andes. The cool winds from the Pacific provide a very long growing season, which allows for terrific terroir for the whites and pinot noir. The improvement in many of its wines has been radical in the last few years.

With large tasting rooms and a wonderful store, this property is an anchor for the growing wine tourism in Chile. Reservations are recommended. hospitality@veramonte.cl

VERAMONTE SAUVIGNON BLANC RESERVA, 2008

COLOR   Clear maize

AROMA   Tropical citrus bouquet; mineral overtones; inviting and suggestive

BODY   Soft and smooth; light, pleasant; aperitif or with shellfish

PALATE   Easy and smooth; muted acidity; citrus and mineral; very even

FINISH   Terrific finish with smooth taste

OUTSTANDING

90,000 Cases, cold maceration, 100% stainless steel, picked at night in very low temperatures, great buy at $12. Every year gets better. *Best-selling Sauvignon Blanc from Chile*

VERAMONTE CHARDONNAY RESERVA 2007

COLOR   Maize
AROMA   Round bouquet of minerals and fruits, sea air
         influence, appealing
BODY   Complex, interesting, delicious, great minerality,
         very smooth
PALATE   Very refreshing, tropical fruits, minerals and
         light sea breeze
FINISH   Lovely, smooth, ideal for grilled bass or sole

OUTSTANDING TO GREAT
25,000 cases, 30% aged in oak, adding a certain texture of smoothness to the
juicy grapes; Paul Hobbs consulted on the Chard and Pinot Noir. Terrific
quality and only $12

VERAMONTE PINOT NOIR RESERVA 2008

COLOR   Crimson
AROMA   Medium bouquet of cherry, berry, minerals;
         very inviting
BODY   Easy to understand, very smooth; medium
PALATE   Lovely soft; taste of berries/minerals, sea
         breeze
FINISH   Long, smooth, delicious

OUTSTANDING
15,000 cases, 70% in new French oak; night harvested and hand sorted;
climate characterized by morning fog and cool winds; long season with
afternoon sun, $15

VERAMONTE RITUAL PINOT NOIR 2008

COLOR   Crimson
AROMA   Inviting mix of berries, minerals and spices;
         elegant
BODY   Medium and very smooth; round; terrific
PALATE   Sea air adds depth to berries, minerals, herbs;
         elegant
FINISH   Smooth, elegant and enjoyable

OUTSTANDING
Special selection, 10,000 cases, first vintage, 100% French oak, cold
maceration, $20

VERAMONTE MERLOT RESERVA 2008

COLOR   Deep crimson
AROMA   Mild bouquet of fruit/minerals,
BODY   Medium, some complexity of minerals, spices on the berries
PALATE Spices come to the fore, very smooth and easy
FINISH   Easy and smooth, velvety

OUTSTANDING
80% in French and American oak, $15

VERAMONTE CABERNET SAUVIGNON RESERVA 2008

COLOR   Dark purple
AROMA   Inviting bouquet of smoky fruit; minerality give complexity
BODY   Medium to full, soft, some complexity; fruits/minerals/spices
PALATE Delicious, smooth
FINISH   Friendly and smooth, delicious

OUTSTANDING
80% in French and American oak, 8 months, 94% Cab, from Colchagua Valley, extended hang time, hand picked, $15

PRIMUS 2006

COLOR   Very dark purple
AROMA   Variety of grapes; inviting and complex; very enticing
BODY   Medium-Full, Carmenere welcome, subtle overtones; spices
PALATE Elegant, fruits, spices, minerals; delicious
FINISH   Smooth and long, silky

GREAT
30,000 cases, Cab, Syrah, Carmenere and Merlot, oak aged for 14 months; very low yield, Napa style; $25
NOTE: Veramonte is coming out with a 2006 Malbec from Carlos Pulenta's extraordinary vineyard, 1000 Cases, at $20. It is magnificent, top of the line from Argentina and will spark controversy. First vintage.

VINA ALTAIR

Altair is a subsidiary of the second largest wine group in Chile, Vina San Pedro Tarapaca. San Pedro traditionally has been a producer of massive wines. Altair is the name of the brightest star in the Aquila constellation

Altair is run independently and is by far the best quality winery in the group. Altair owns 150 hectares, of which 72 are planted. The terraces of vineyards are from almost 2000 feet to over 2500 feet above sea level in the foothills of the Andes (Alto Cachopal). The vinification is traditional, and artesenal. With handmade selection of the grapes, and a very low yield, everything is done to preserve the terroir of the special vineyards. Altair is vinified in traditional Bordeaux wooden vats, Sideral only in stainless steel. The wine is aged from 12 months to 18 in French oak barrels.

The winery offers three different tours, two of which are horseback tours of from 1.5 to 4 hours. Some go up the mountains, with appetizers and wine being served. On nights with a full moon, the rides are very dramatic. The highlight is a half-day experience, with a horse ride up to Alto de Aquila, some 2200 feet above sea level, with lunch and the icon wines, topped off by breathtaking views of the valleys. Lunch and dinner with reservations can be enjoyed at the quincho of the winery. Reservations essential. tours@altairwines.com; info@altairwine.com; www.altairwines.com

ALTAIR SIDERAL 2004

COLOR   Very Intense Violet
AROMA   Extremely Round, Full and inviting.
BODY   Big, bold, Lots of Berries and minerals
PALATE Smooth and very delicious
FINISH Silky smooth

GREAT

Predominantly 75% Cabernet Sauvignon, Merlot and Carmenere are around 15%, touches of Cab Franc, Syrah and Sangiovese. Superb, the winemakers vary the blend depending on each year's crop. 15,000 cases. 50% new French oak, 50% second use, all for 12 to 15 months. 2002 and 2003 also are outstanding and aging well. 2004 is the best vintage yet. Incredible value at $25.

ALTAIR 2004

COLOR   Very Intense Violet
AROMA   Round and Full; inviting bouquet of berries
BODY   Full, Elegant, Sophisticated, very smooth and
        Round
PALATE Silky, velvety, majestic; Bordeaux-like; Dark
        berries/minerals
FINISH Long, languid; smooth and delicious

GREAT

86% Cabernet Sauvignon, supported by Carmenere and
Merlot; an Icon from Chile. Only 3500 cases; blind taste
this against your favorite wine. Again, 2004 is the best
vintage yet, although 2002 (the first) and 2003 are aging fabulously well. $75
For any serious collector of South American wines

VINA LA ROSA

One of oldest wineries in Chile, Vina La Rosa was established in 1824, having been purchased from the first President of Chile by the ancestor of today's company president. The Ossa family seal is still present after almost two centuries of viticulture and winemaking.

Don Ismael Ossa Errazuriz, the current chairman (since 1987) of Vina La Rosa, is the 6th generation to direct the operation and his family owns about 72% of the company's shares. With 806 hectares, the company produces over 500,000 cases annually. Up until 16 years ago, most of the wine produced In these vineyards were sold to Concha Y Toro. Since, the winery is bottling under its own name.

Located in some of the prime vineyards of Chile, La Rosa is just south of Santiago,, tucked into the fertile Cachapoal Valley, between the Pacific Ocean and the Andes, with the Cachapoal River running across the valley toward the Ocean. Some of the vineyards are surrounded by coastal mountains on one side and the Andes on the other. There is a charming guest house and restaurant no longer open to the public. It should be restored and take its place as a historically important site. Tours by appointment. www.larosa.cl

LA ROSA LA PALMA CARMENERE RESERVA 2008

COLOR   Deep Purple
AROMA   Round, inviting bouquet of grapes and mnerals
BODY   Very full,, smooth, terrific taste;
PALATE   Delicious, Full taste, Smooth
FINISH   Excellent, long and smooth

OUTSTANDING
100% Carmenere, aged for 6 months in oak, 12,000 cases, Incredible value at only $12

LA ROSA LA PALMA CABERNET SAUVIGNON RESERVA 2008

COLOR   Deep Purple
AROMA   Inviting berry bouquet complimented by
         Minerals and spices
BODY   Medium to Full, Lots of Fruit, needs to breathe
         and open
PALATE   Big tannins, minerals, somewhat complex, good
         structure
FINISH   Smooth, big fruits, but still subtle in texture

OUTSTANDING

85% Cab, 15% Carmenere, 5% Cab Franc, with various layers of dark berries from the Carmenere grapes, this Cabernet is more more complex and interesting than it normally is.

LA CAPITANA CARMENERE 2008

COLOR   Almost Black
AROMA   Full, inviting bouquet of black berries and spice
BODY   Full and complex, lots currant berry, minerals
PALATE   Very sensual and strong; smooth
FINISH   Rolls off the tongue, long and very full

OUTSTANDING

100% Carmenere, aged in oak for 11 months; La Capitania is a name for the majestic palm trees, found on the Palmeira plantation, 15,000 cases, another incredible value. Must have patience and allow to breathe for 30 minutes minimum to fully appreciate. The La Capitania Cab, blend and Merlot bottles are three outstanding wines as well and at the same price they are true steals. $173

LA ROSA CUVEE DON RECA 2007

COLOR   Very deep Purple
AROMA   Inviting, almost french in bouquet of
                berries and minerals
BODY   Full, Very smooth and full of
                character and charm
PALATE   Subtle and delicious; smooth as silk
FINISH   Long and spectacular with hype; very smooth and elegant

GREAT

aged in 100% new French oak for 1 year, 7000 cases, blend of merlot and Cab, with some Syrah and Carmenere, a spectacular example of fine winemaking and only $26. Truly superb

OSSA 2004

COLOR   Intense Violet
AROMA   Deceivingly simple bouquet, subtle
BODY   Full and fruity, Smooth as silk, now
                overpowering
PALATE   Smooth and round; complex, Berries and
                minerals
FINISH   Clear, smooth and delicious

GREAT

blend of Cab, Carmenere, Merlot, Syrah and Cab Franc with a tendency for the Carmenere to take on greater importance, 18 months in new French oak, no filtering, fining, clearing, only 1000 cases, 2004 was not a great year; expect the great 2007's for this icon to be even better; $100 Among the top wines of Chile

VIU MANENT

Founded in 1935, Viu Manent is a family business with its third generation of Viu family management. A little over two hours by car to the South of Santiago, Viu Manent possesses 260 hectares (642 acres). Today, the winery produces 170,000 cases, with 93% being exported. The U.S. is the primary destination, with Brazil right behind.

Grant Phelps, a native of New Zealand, is the talented wine maker who is making his mark with his special approach to the blended leading brands of Viu Manent. Viu Manent has made its fame as Chile's largest producer of Malbec wines, with plantations in Colchagua Valley. It also makes an Argentine Malbec, VIBO with grapes from Uco Valley in Mendoza, Argentina. Their portfolio begins on the varietal level, passing through the reservas and finishing up with the Flagship Icon, Viu 1.

Viu Manent is located in the heart of Colchagua Valley and is very tourist friendly, being one of the most visited wineries in Colchagua Valley. With 2 distinct restaurants, one with gourmet Chilean fare, in a rustic but sophisticated, colonial setting, the other outside in the courtyard, with a more common-man approach, featuring assados or grilled meat, barbecue style. The excellent store and tasting area features the winery's complete line of wines, as well as Chilean arts and crafts.

Viu Manent also offers horse and carriage rides from its outstanding Equestrian club, which is open to the public. Visitors can take a buggy ride through parts of the vineyard. Other wine related activities can also be had. www.viumanent.cl; export@viumanent.cl

VIU MANENT EL OLIVAR ALTO SYRAH SINGLE VINEYARD 2007

COLOR   Violet
AROMA   Enticing bouquet of dark berries
BODY   Medium to Full, Some complexity
PALATE Round, layers of fruit, smooth,
FINISH Smooth, long, easy

VERY GOOD TO OUTSTANDING
94% Syrah, 6% Petit Verdot, 18 months in oak, $25

VIU MANENT CABERNET SAUVIGNON LA CAPILLA ESTATE 2007

COLOR   Intense Violet
AROMA   Alluring bouquet of blackberries muted by oak
BODY   Full, Very Round, well structured, balanced
PALATE Smooth, well rounded tannins, dark cherry
        overtones
FINISH Smooth, long

OUTSTANDING (IF AGED LONGER MIGHT BE GREAT)
14% Malbec, rest Cab, Terrific wine that would be close to perfect if aged longer, 14 months in new oak, $25

VIU MANENT CARMENERE RESERVA 2008

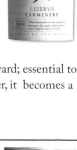

COLOR   Deep Purple
AROMA   Full Bouquet of Fruit and spices
BODY   Full (after 40 minutes opened), Complex,
        Wonderful spices
PALATE Round, structured, terrific Carmenere
FINISH Smooth Velvety, long

OUTSTANDING TO GREAT
100% Carmenere, 10,000 cases, most important wine for vineyard; essential to breathe minimum of 40 minutes, before that wine is tight; after, it becomes a terrific wine, 11 months in oak, a steal at $15.

VIU 1 2007

COLOR   Deep Purple
AROMA   Alluring, fruity bouquet
BODY   Full, Round, Red Cherry overtones, with spices
        and minerals
PALATE Smooth, Layers of fruit, muted by oak, well-
        balanced
FINISH Smooth and creamy, excellent

OUTSTANDING
94% Carmenere, 6% Petit Verdot, 1000 cases, very low yield, single vineyard Colchagua plantation, numbered bottles adds charm, 22 months in French oak, Flagship wine, $70

WINE TOURISM – ARGENTINA

Wines are intimately related to the geography and history of the country. Mendoza region is the heart and soul of winemaking for Argentina and presents fascinating microclimates to be visited and enjoyed. Patagonia and Salta are the other two very important regions, with excellent hotels and restaurants and fascinating geography and climate.

There are many wine tourism groups in Argentina. The one in Mendoza that I have found to be very reliable, as well as creative and well priced, is VINTURA Gourmet Wine and Adventure travel. Veronica Mausbach is its owner, vmausbach@vintura.com.ar

Many wineries have very good to great restaurants. Some have small posadas (inns). Most wineries have tours, and a good number have extremely well-organized ones involving the tourist in aspects of wine making. Tours can be arranged at each winery with the information supplied in its review earlier in the book. Reservations are essential. Here are some posadas and restaurants that I found to be most interesting.

POSADAS
Wine aficionados should make every attempt to stay in a posada or two on their trip.

MENDOZA
CLUB TAPIZ
Club Tapiz is a tourist-oriented winery with a complete infrastructure. Just 20 minutes from downtown, it has touches of luxury, with a pool, workout area and restaurant. The 1890 architecture has been preserved.

SALENTEIN
Posada Salentein is a lovely, relaxing mountain inn that overlooks large vineyards at the foot of the Andes. The restaurant has magnificent views. The winery has a very avant-garde art gallery and a permanent collection of fascinating artwork. The architecture of the winery offers striking angles and features local arts and crafts and native stonework. The gourmet restaurant excels with Argentine cuisine.

CHATEAU ANCON
Chateau Ancon offers a sophisticated alternative in the Tupungato region at the feet of the Andes. In a large castle, the Inn offers gourmet criolla food, horseback tours, parks for strolls, and creative architecture by one of Argentina's leading artists.

LARS DE CHACARA

Lares de Chacara is a quaint winery inn about 20 minutes from downtown. Located in a sophisticated village where many locals get away for the weekend, this is an upscale alternative.

VISTALBA

Pousada Carlos Pulenta at the Vistalba winery is a small, very sophisticated Inn in one of the top modern wineries. Recently inaugurated, the posada is located in a 53-hectare plantation with an outstanding Franco Argentine restaurant.

O. FOURNIER

O Fournier is a modern winery from a Spanish winemaking family that offers a simple inn and a fantastic restaurant. The tasting rooms are a few floors up with tremendous views of the Andes and the restaurant is in a modern structure, seemingly from outer space. Located almost two hours from downtown Mendoza, this location is a special treat.

SALTA AND CAFAYATE VALLEY

There are many picturesque inns and posadas in the Salta region, a magnificent area with five major vineyards and vistas of the Andes that will take your breath away.

PATIOS DE CAFAYATE

A 30-room, five-star venture run by Starwood Hotels on the property of El Esteco winery, known better to foreigners as Michel Torino. Very sophisticated with a terrific restaurant and spa, this hotel offers a true getaway from everything in the rest of the world. With magnificent views, high altitude and a great microclimate, one can drink great wines, feast on local food and have a total "relax" an hour and a half from Salta by car.

ESTANCIA DE COLOME

A small posada in the Northern mountains, owned by the Hess family, offers comfortable quarters, a first-class restaurant, and horseback riding tours, inter alia. For a romantic getaway, the wine tour is first class and the wines terrific. From the wines to the sheep, everything is organic. Two hours from Salta. info@estanciacolome.com; info@bodegacolome.com

RESTAURANTS

Mendoza has a number of terrific restaurants located in wineries that open only for lunch.

Those on a leisurely schedule should include a winery tour followed by a gourmet lunch with terrific wines, perhaps preceded by a wine tasting to choose one's favorites. There are numerous terrific restaurants within the various sub-sections of the region for tourism throughout the Mendoza area. For more information, go the reviews of each winery earlier in the book.

FINCA DECERO

A magnificent modern winery with outstanding wines, Finca Decero has a gourmet restaurant with breathtaking views of the vineyards and the Andes. With an excellent wine-tasting program and shop, this is a must see for its food, wines, views and architecture. info@decero.com; decero@decero.com

VISTALABA

Located amongst 53 magnificent hectares, La Bourgogne is a *tres chic* restaurant at Finca Carlos Pulenta. Modern architecture, terrific wines, great views of the vineyards and the Andes mountains, along with delicious Franco-Argentine food makes this visit a real treat.

O. FOURNIER

Housed in a winery built like a UFO, this fantastic restaurant is a must see in the Uco Valley region. With very creative cuisine, the breathtaking views are a show in themselves. Wonderful wines, service and exquisite food from a kitchen directed by the founder's wife, O Fournier should not be missed. The winery and its wines are named after stars seen in the Southern Hemisphere. Open only for lunch, O Fournier has a sister restaurant in downtown Mendoza that serves dinner.

1884-FRANCIS MALLMAN

One of the great restaurants of Mendoza, located in the winery of Bodega Caro, minutes from downtown, 1884 offers lunch and dinner under the stars – it almost never rains in Mendoza. With a beautiful bar, wonderful food and service, and a wine list to die for, this is a not-to-be-missed gourmet experience.

BODEGAS SALENTEIN

With an emphasis on everything Argentine, there are 2 restaurants offering criolla food in a spectacular, modern structure at the feet of the Andes. Separate from the winery, the restaurant is an ideal option after one of the various tours offered here.

BODEGA NORTON

One of the oldest wineries in Mendoza, Bodega Norton has a picturesque restaurant with very sophisticated, delicious food and a terrific selection of wines. The winery offers very creative tours and has an excellent store to taste and buy a variety of products. A terrific program of wine participation and delicious lunch makes for a wonderful wine experience.

NIETO SENETINER

With many creative tours, the winery has a nice restaurant and store, with views of the vineyards and the Andes mountains. Winemaking tours are its specialty and the location is historic and beautiful.

BODEGA TAPIZ

The sophisticated infrastructure includes an interesting restaurant located amidst beautiful gardens in an active winery. A full shop and inn complement a wonderful lunch.

FAMILIA ZUCCARDI—CASA DEL VISITANTE

The Zuccardi winery is a traditional tourist stop on the Mendoza tours that offers the visitor a varied series of wine experiences as well as a nice family restaurant. With one of the largest tourist infrastructures in Mendoza, the visitor has a vast choice of tour alternatives as well as a delicious meal.

WINE TOURISM – CHILE

Wine defines a great deal of the tourism industry in Chile. With the exception of the extreme cold in the south of Chile, the various microclimates we have described herein harbor fabulous vineyards as well as many tourist attractions.

We will highlight the locations that we consider the most interesting. This is not intended as a complete list, but should touch on many of the outstanding locations. Interesting fact: the most important tourist attraction in Chile by number of visitors is Concha y Toro's winery in Maipo, about 30 minutes from Santiago.

There are many terrific restaurants in the wine districts, especially the areas within two hours of Santiago. All are open for lunch, some for dinner. An excellent tourism agency that specializes in wine tours is Turisvino, which is based in Santiago. www.turisvino.com

POSADAS

RESIDENCE LAPOSTOLLE
One of the jewels of Chile, this small inn on top of the winery of Lapostolle requires planning, as there are only four spacious rooms and a wonderful restaurant, both with views of the Apalta Valley and the Andes mountains. Sophisticated and charming, it can be used as a base to see the other magnificent wineries in the region. Expensive. www.lapostolle.com; info@lapostolle.com

VINA MATETIC Bed and Breakfast
Located just 45 minutes from Santiago and near Valparaiso as well, this is an upscale, very comfortable inn, with an outstanding restaurant, Equilibrio. Located in the San Antonio Valley, Matetic is an ultra modern winery with very good wines. Extremely tourist friendly, it has wonderful tasting areas and an active wine shop. Its wines are certified organic, with 9000 hectares of planted vineyards. info@mateticvineyards.com; www.matetic.com

CASA SILVA
Please see the section on Casa Silva, which is a wonderful, historic vineyard with a very comfortable, upscale inn that has large, clean rooms in what used to be the manor house of the estate. An equestrian center, polo field, and rodeo arena complement the delicious food of the restaurant and cigar/wine bar. Colchagua Valley, about two hours from Santiago. casasilva@casasilva.cl; www.casasilva.com

CASA REAL
Santa Rita is one of the oldest wineries in Chile and the Casa Real is the former manor house of the estate. A charming colonial structure with large rooms and a comfortable restaurant, Casa Real is luxurious and inviting. Additional

attractions are the wine tours and the museum with the owner's wonderful collections of pre-Colombian art. www.santarita.com

VINA SANTA CRUZ
Begun in 1999 in the Colchagua Valley, about two hours by car from Santiago, Vina Santa Cruz is a tourist-oriented location with many wine educational tours and a hotel and casino. The hotel offers full services and is a useful center for seeing the Colchagua Valley wineries. www.hotelsantacruzplaza.cl

RESTAURANTS

EQUILIBRIO
Housed in the modern architecture of Matetic winery, Equilibrio features organic gourmet food, using Chilean style preparations. A delicious lunch completes the tours of this magnificent winery.

CASA SILVA
Rich with tradition, there are two restaurants to choose from, one in a wine bar with light snacks, and a full gourmet treat upstairs. Both overlook a beautiful barrel room and feature the great wines from Casa Silva. One of the rare restaurants open for dinner as well as lunch.

CONCHA Y TORO
Surprisingly well priced, this delicious location is in the heart of the terrific winery and features traditional Chilean fare. Concha y Toro is very tourist friendly, steeped in tradition and a great outing for the family. Include some time in the wonderful shop as well.

VIU MANENT
Viu Manent is an unusual tourist attraction, with two totally different restaurants and a plethora of tours. Extremely tourist friendly, the barbeque restaurant is outdoors and very low key. Inside, a gourmet restaurant features upscale Chilean dishes and fabulous wines.

RESIDENCE LAPOSTOLLE
A delicious Franco-Chileno gourmet restaurant open only to the guests of the residence. Expensive but fantastique! info@lapostolle.com

VERAMONTE
The winery offers tours and food and wine pairings that are very interesting. An extensive wine tasting room and shop add to the experience. www.veramonte.com

SANTA RITA
Santa Rita's Dona Paula restaurant features traditional Chilean fare and is exquisite. Combined with tours and tastings, as well a fascinating museum, this location is a wonderful day trip. www.santarita.com